SUSTAINABLE STYLE

ALEXANDRA BRUCE &
CAROLINE AKSELSON

SUSTAINABLE STYLE

27 GARMENTS TO SEW FOR A MORE CONSIDERED CLOSET

PHOTOGRAPHY BY
BROOKE HARWOOD

Hardie Grant

QUADRILLE

Contents

Patrick Grant

I have in my wardrobe many pieces of clothing that are over half a century old – jackets from my grandfather, overcoats from my godfather, and various suits that I inherited from my father, including a dinner suit that dates back to 1935. They are special to me. Use and the passage of time have only increased their value. They have been made malleable and been moulded by use, while wear and the odd repair have added character to their once uniform appearance – all of which, in my eyes, only serves to increase their beauty. Their very fibres are infused with the history of the places they have been and the events at which they have been worn.

Every piece of clothing deserves to be cherished; worn, repaired, passed on and eventually recycled. A century ago we'd have paid a week's wages for a dress and worn it for years. When an item of clothing was worn out, the precious textile would have been reclaimed and something new would have been made from it, and the cycle would have started all over again. And it wasn't just clothing that we cherished: anything that was made from textiles, from bed linen to curtains, was treated with respect. Repurposing was commonplace. Everything we owned was valued.

But today, when it's more important than ever that we slow down our consumption, the amount of clothing that we buy and throw away has never been greater. Rampant consumption tied to ever-lower prices means that we are fast depleting the earth's natural resources and our industrial activities are polluting our planet on a scale never seen before. A great many of the people who labour to create our clothes are treated with a lack of human decency.

But we can all choose to act differently. As individuals we have the power to encourage and enact positive change.

If you watch *The Great British Sewing Bee*, then it's likely that you know more about textiles and clothing than the average person. You are very well placed to be an actor in this change. Make the simple decision to slow down your consumption, buy fewer but better pieces, invest in clothes made from the best natural fabrics, made by people paid a fair wage. Repair your clothes, learn to love a darn and a patch, alter them, pass them on. And when they wear out, take that precious fabric and make something new from it.

Waste nothing. Value everything.

I sincerely hope that this book can inspire you, and give you practical help in achieving this aim.

Esme Young

Even though I've spent my working life in the fashion industry, I never cease to be amazed by the contestants on *The Great British Sewing Bee*. They epitomize everything I love about sewing – great technical skills, tremendous creativity, a love of beautiful fabrics and a willingness to learn from and share their ideas with others. They are amateurs in the truest sense of the word – people who love what they do and who put their hearts and souls into their creations – and I think that's what resonates with the viewing public.

The Great British Sewing Bee is also a testament to the huge renaissance in sewing in recent years. Once seen by many people as something that you only did if you couldn't afford to buy ready-made clothes, sewing is now viewed as an empowering and creative craft. Master a few basic techniques and you can not only make clothes that fit you perfectly but also create totally individual garments that express your personality and style.

Hand in hand with this is a growing awareness of the importance of sustainability in fashion. People are turning away from the 'throw away' culture of fast fashion that's prevailed for so long. Instead, they're looking for clothes that will last and that will have a minimal effect on the environment, whether that's in the way the fabric is produced or by refashioning 'pre-loved' garments into something new and exciting.

The Great British Sewing Bee has embraced this philosophy wholeheartedly. For me, one of the highlights of the series has always been the 90-minute transformation challenges – and boy, have we given our contestants some weird and wonderful challenges over the years! I relish their inventiveness and the way their individual styles shine through, even when they're up against the most severe of time constraints. So, in addition to a wide range of projects, from a simple wrap skirt to a '50s-style tea dress, or a versatile jumpsuit to a man's linen jacket, this book also includes a number of 'transformations' that turn battered old

jeans or vintage household linens into new garments or accessories. I hope that, like the challenges on the television series, they'll encourage you to repurpose items from your wardrobe, or even search out secondhand treasures online or in charity shops, in order to give new life to items that might otherwise be destined for landfill.

So whether you're an experienced sewer or completely new to this wonderful craft, I hope you'll find both inspiration and a host of useful tips and techniques in this latest addition to the *Sewing Bee* canon.

Introduction

Since the first season of *The Great British Sewing Bee*, the individual, solitary activity of sewing has turned into a hobby that connects our sewing nooks all over the world. The show, and also the rise of visibility of sewing on social media, has done great things to promote sewing. *The Great British Sewing Bee* brought sewing back into the spotlight as a hobby for everyone and dusted off the image it had in previous years. When someone tells you, 'I love your dress', you can now proudly respond, 'thank you, I made it'.

This book is aimed at confident home sewers. We will assume you have basic skills and will not go through the basic techniques, although you will find information on more advanced or specialist techniques, such as shirring and inserting a fly zip, where necessary. It is accompanied by 14 downloadable PDF patterns, some of which you may be familiar with from the television series and some of which are brand new. All are classic, timeless designs. Several can be adapted so that you can make different garments from the same pattern: you can make the top half of the summer dress on page 88 as a blouse, for example, or sew the sleep set (page 62) as an all-in-one romper. We've also created the patterns in a wider range of sizes than most sewing books – US sizes 4 to 18 for women, and 34 to 44 for men – and on page 30, you will find details of how to alter the patterns to create a perfect fit.

At a time when people are increasingly aware of the impact their actions have on the environment, it's crucial that sustainability is entwined with your sewing. Caring more for the garments we make, and those we already own, is a small step we can take towards a more considered wardrobe.

Throughout the book there are lots of tips and tricks that you can introduce to make your sewing more sustainable, whether that's by choosing fabric produced in an environmentally friendly way, using offcuts to minimise waste, re-using buttons, zips and other haberdashery items from clothes that really are too far gone to save, or even the way you launder your clothes. Amongst the projects, we've also included a number of quick-and-easy transformations that will hopefully inspire you to recycle garments and even household linen that you already own.

Sewing has become a popular pastime for people of all ages, wanting to create something with their hands, desiring to sew what they can't find in the shops, or interested in making sure they know where something comes from. We want to have creative control of what we make and, most of all, we sew to suit our bodies and our individual personalities, rather than what society or trends tell us we should wear. With the rise of fast fashion and 'throw-away' culture, makers of today are concerned more than ever with the ethics of fashion, wanting to make stylish clothes that will last and be cherished.

Throughout the book you will find different techniques for the same thing (such as setting in one-piece sleeves in two ways) and more specialist insights (such as a detailed look at button stands). We would like to encourage you to try these different techniques, as there are many ways to get the same result, so that you can judge for yourself which techniques are suitable in which circumstances, or simply which ones you prefer!

How to use this book

PATTERNS TO ACCOMPANY THE BOOK

This book includes 14 downloadable PDF patterns nested in multiple sizes. The women's patterns come in sizes US 4–18 and the men's patterns in US 34–44. These patterns can be downloaded at hardiegrant. com/uk/quadrille/sustainable-style in A4 or A0 for you to print at home or print full-size at a copy shop.

Once printed and pieced together, cut around or trace your pattern onto dressmaker's tracing paper before cutting out, make sure you follow the lines for your size, following the instructions on page 30. You may find that your actual body measurements fall between two pattern sizes; turn to page 32 for information on how to 'grade' patterns between sizes.

The majority of our patterns come with additional cutting lines for different sleeve, skirt and trouser lengths, providing you with more choice when sewing your wardrobe. You will also find information on adjusting patterns to fit your body shape on pages 32–37.

....

TOP TIP

In the step-by-step illustrations accompanying the projects, the right of the fabric is shown as a dark tone and the wrong side as a light tone.

....

LAY PLANS

The lay plans included in this book indicate how each project should be cut out – where the grain line on the pattern should be placed, whether pieces should be cut on the fold or not. Although fabrics comes in widths ranging from 115 to 150 cm/45 to 60 in. (see page 47), wider widths are generally best for dressmaking. However, where the pattern pieces will comfortably fit on fabric that is 115 cm (45 in.) wide, we've included lay plans for two fabric widths. Lay plans are designed to help you cut the fabric in the most economical way possible, to minimise wastage. We have provided the lay plans for the patterns to be cut on the fold, to give you an estimate of how much fabric you need; however, it's worth noting that cutting on the fold isn't always the most economical: cutting all pieces on a single layer of fabric can sometimes save you fabric.

Check each lay plan when pinning your pattern pieces to your fabric.

The majority of the projects in this book are to be cut with the fabric folded in half right side to right side, with the selvedges together. This is so that, when you cut out your pattern pieces, you have two perfectly matching pieces. It also ensures that any pattern markings are on the inside of your garment.

Occasionally you are required to cut the fabric flat, and not on the fold. This is the case when a pattern piece is wider than the folded fabric. This is shown in the lay plan if applicable.

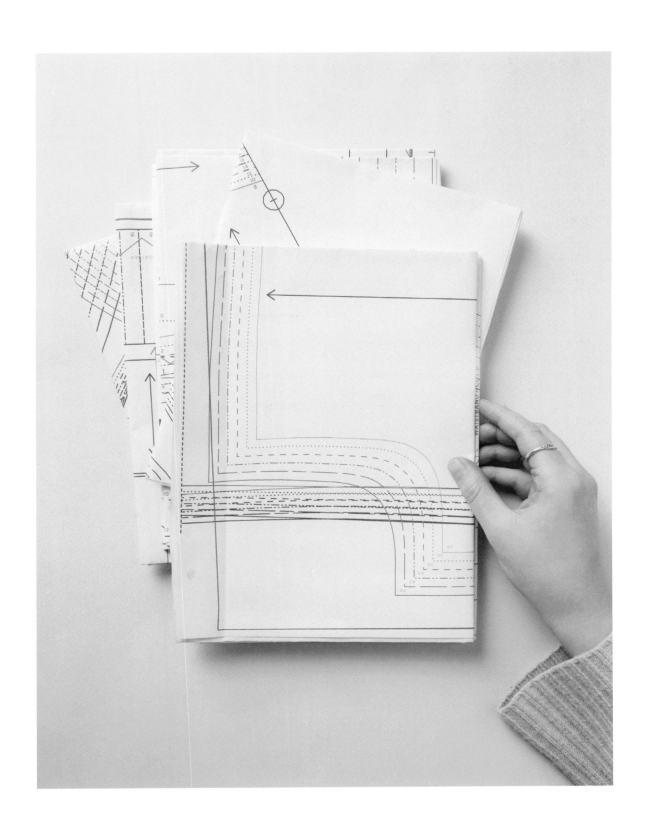

DIFFICULTY LEVELS

Each project in this book is given a difficulty level – beginners, intermediate or advanced. If you are a beginner, we recommend that you start with a project such as the Sleep Set (page 62) or the Midi Wrap Skirt (page 74).

PATTERN MARKINGS AND TERMINOLOGY

The pattern sheets included with the book are marked with indications such as how many of each piece you need to cut out for your project, bust darts, waist darts, grain lines and notches.

Once you learn what each symbol or lines means, you will find dressmaking so much easier. When you have cut out your fabric pieces, but before you remove the paper patterns, you will need to transfer the markings to your fabric – see page 23.

General information

Each pattern piece includes the pattern number, sizes on that particular piece, what the piece is (e.g. FRONT), and simple cutting directions such as, 'CUT 2 FABRIC, CUT 1 INTERFACING'.

Grain line arrows

Usually these will have arrowheads at one or both ends. These lines are pinned parallel to the selvedge to ensure the pattern piece is correctly angled and cut out.

Angled grain line

'Place to fold' lines have a right-angled arrowhead at either end to indicate that the pattern piece should be put on the fold of fabric.

Notches

These are short, straight lines on the cutting line extending into the seam allowance. They are used to match up seams, fronts to backs, sleeves to armholes. Cut these notches outwards from the cutting line and into the seam allowance, so that you don't cut inside of where the finished seam will be.

Lengthen or shorten lines

These are two parallel lines that indicate where the pattern can be made longer or shorter without distorting the garment shape.

Solid lines within the pattern

These indicate buttonhole positions and may also indicate the location of bust line, waist line and hip line.

Circles

These are used to mark the ends of openings such as zips, or the end of stitch lines such as gathers. They also mark placement of details such as darts, tabs, belt loops and pockets.

Cross

This symbol can mark the point of a dart, highlight the start and end of a particular feature such as a smocking line, or indicate the centre of a button.

Zigzag line

This line shows where to gather.

Darts

Are shown as V-shaped lines extending from the cutting line into the garment. To sew, match the two lines of the V, folding the fabric with right sides together, and stitch along the line from the widest point to the tip. Darts shape fabric to fit over body contours.

Parallel lines with circles and an arrow line at the bottom

These lines indicate the position of tucks and pleats. One line is the fold line, the other the placement line. The arrowhead indicates which direction to take the fold. To make pleats, fold the fabric from the fold line to the placement line, then press. Tack across the top of the pleats to hold them in place.

Cutting lines

The outside lines on the pattern pieces are the cutting lines. Different sizes have different line types such as solid, dotted or dashed, which are also numbered by size. In some areas the lines merge, so it is advisable to go over your size line with a coloured pencil before tracing.

Women's sizing

——————————————— 4

· · · · · · · · · · · · · · · · · · · 6

— — — — — — — 8

—— · —— ·· —— ·· —— · 10

— — — — — — — — 12

—— ——— —— ——— —— ——— —— 14

— —— — — — 16

——————————————— 18

Men's sizing

——————————————— 34

· · · · · · · · · · · · · · · · · · · 36

— — — — — — — 38

—— · —— ·· —— · —— · 40

— —— — — 42

——————————————— 44

Sewing kit

Sewing is a wonderful activity that requires lots of different tools. The tools you need depends on what kind of sewing you end up doing: a small set of tools will be sufficient if you are mending and repairing only, whereas dressmaking from scratch will require significantly more. There are many varieties of most tools, so don't be tempted to buy everything at once because you may not like all of them or end up using them. After a while you will know what you like and you will have established your own basic kit. If you are doing a technique that requires a specialist tool but you don't think you would get enough use out of it in the future, see if you can borrow it from someone rather than buying your own for a single occasion.

Basic sewing kit

These are what we consider to be the essential tools for dressmaking. There are other, more specialist pieces of kit available and, if a project requires a piece of equipment that's not mentioned below, we've listed it separately in the project instructions.

MEASURING TOOLS

Careful measuring is essential at every stage. In fact, the saying goes 'measure twice, cut once'!

Tape measure

Used to measure yourself as well as your sewing projects, this is one of the most essential items in your sewing kit. A tape measure becomes less accurate over time as it stretches, so it's a good idea to replace it every once in a while.

French curve and/or pattern master

A French curve, which is a ruler with a curved end as well as a straight edge, is used for drafting sewing patterns and adapting printed sewing patterns, particularly for grading in between sizes or trueing pattern lines. A pattern master is extremely useful if you draft your own patterns, as it has everything you need for pattern making in one tool.

Seam allowance gauge

This little contraption will help you achieve perfectly even hems and seams. It's like a mini ruler with specific measurements that you can use to achieve an even seam allowance, a neat hem, or perfectly positioned buttonholes.

MARKING TOOLS

You will need a selection of marking tools to transfer marks from patterns to fabric. There is a large variety available, and it's very much a matter of personal preference as to which ones to use.

Tailor's chalk or dressmaker's chalk pencils

This is the traditional choice, as the marks can be easily brushed out. Both chalk slabs and pencils come in a range of colours (white, blue, yellow), so choose the one that will show up best on your fabric.

Air- and water-soluble pens

Marks made with an air-soluble pen simply disappear after a while. Water-soluble pens are a more recent innovation and have the advantage that the marks cannot be brushed off accidentally. Please note that these will only be useful on projects that will be washed.

Dressmaker's carbon paper and tracing wheel

Dressmaker's carbon paper comes in a variety of colours and is used to transfer pattern outlines and indications such as darts, pleats and notches onto fabric. It is used in conjunction with a tracing wheel; you can get very spiky wheels, medium wheels and wheels with no spikes at all.

CUTTING TOOLS

Sharp cutting tools are essential – not only will they produce neater lines, but they will also be gentler on your hands. Look after your scissors. Blunt scissors don't achieve clean cutting lines, so make sure to sharpen them if they have reached that stage. You can have this done for you or purchase a scissor sharpener.

Dressmaking shears

A pair of good-quality dressmaking shears will last you for years if you take care of them. Use dressmaking shears that are at least 20 cm (8 in.) long for cutting out your dressmaking projects. Have your scissors sharpened once a year.

Snips

A pair of snips, or embroidery scissors, is great for cutting loose thread ends, so keep them next to you as you sew.

Rotary cutter

This tool is great for cutting out fabrics that are trickier to handle, such as very fine fabrics and stretch fabrics, as you don't have to disturb the fabric once you have laid it out. Make sure your blade is sharp. You can get different sizes of blades depending on whether you are doing lots of curved lines (you will need a smaller blade) or straighter lines (you'll need a bigger blade). Always use a rotary cutter on a self-healing cutting mat.

Paper scissors

Keep a separate pair of scissors for cutting out your paper patterns. Never, ever use your dressmaking shears on paper, as they will blunt.

Pinking shears

Pinking shears were a traditional cutting tool and often used for neatening seam allowances. However, they are not very practical: once they go blunt, you cannot sharpen them.

PINS AND WEIGHTS

To stop your pattern pieces from slipping out of position as you cut them out, you need to secure them to the fabric.

Dressmaking pins

Good-quality pins are a must. You have a choice of glass-headed pins, regular pins, plastic-headed pins and even novelty pins. Be sure to replace your pins when they become blunt or start to snag your fabrics.

....

TOP TIP

Opt for glass-headed pins rather than plastic-headed pins. Not only are they a more sustainable choice, but they don't melt if you iron over them.

....

Pin magnet

A modern alternative to a pincushion, a pin magnet makes it easy to gather up loose pins from the floor and your work desk.

Pattern weights

Pattern weights hold down your fabric and pattern, and are a quicker and easier solution than pinning. They are great to use on delicate fabrics such as silk if you want to avoid pin marks and they work well with stretch fabrics such as jerseys if you are using a rotary cutter to cut out. Weights are not suitable if you are going to use scissors.

SEWING EQUIPMENT

It goes without saying that you'll need a sewing machine. They range from simple models that do little more than straight and zigzag stitch and maybe an automatic buttonhole, to elaborate machines with lots of fancy embroidery stitches. The projects in this book can all be made with a relatively simple machine, although there are a few essential accessories.

Show your sewing machine some love by regularly getting rid of any fluff or thread caught up inside the machine and by oiling the internal parts surrounding the bobbin. With experience you will be able to hear when the machine is dry and needs some oil, but it's best to not let it get that far. A new machine will typically come with a small bottle of machine oil and after that has finished you can easily buy some more. Make sure you run some scrap fabric through the machine after you have oiled it to catch any excess oil before you start on a new project.

Sewing machine needles

There are many different types and sizes of sewing machine needles you will need in your sewing kit. The chart on the right will will help you choose the right size of sewing machine needle for your fabric. Needles for domestic sewing machines are universal, meaning they will fit any sewing machine brand. You will need different kinds of needles for industrial sewing machines, and also different needles for overlockers. In addition to the different sizes of needles in the chart, you might also need to use a ballpoint needle for stretch fabrics, a twin needle for decorative topstitching or finishing hems on knit fabrics, and a topstitching needle.

....

TOP TIP

Be sure to change your sewing machine needle regularly. It simply gets blunt after a while and won't stitch as neatly.

....

American needle size	European needle size	Fabric weight	Fabric types
8	60	Very fine	Fine silk, chiffon, organza, voile, fine lace
9	65	Very fine	Fine silk, chiffon, organza, voile, fine lace
10	70	Very fine	Fine silk, chiffon, organza, voile, fine lace
11	75	Lightweight	Cotton voile, silk, muslin, spandex, Lycra
12	80	Standard	Cotton, synthetics, spandex, Lycra
14	90	Medium-weight	Denim, corduroy, multiple layers
16	100	Heavy-weight	Heavy denim, heavy corduroy, leather
18	110	Very heavy	Upholstery fabric, leather
20	120	Extra heavy	Heavy upholstery fabric, thick leather, vinyl

Sewing machine feet

Your sewing machine most likely came with all the sewing machine feet you will need. These are the feet we recommend you start with:

- Regular foot
- Invisible zip foot
- Zip foot
- Gathering foot
- Buttonhole foot
- Walking foot

Overlocker

An overlocker is used to finish and trim the seams of your garment, giving them a neat finish that also prevents the fabric from unravelling. A three-thread overlocker is used for neatening seam allowances, whereas jersey fabrics and sportswear should be sewn on a four-thread overlocker for extra strength. However, an overlocker isn't essential; you can also neaten seams on your sewing machine using zigzag stitch (see page 26).

HAND SEWING EQUIPMENT

Although there isn't a lot of hand sewing in the projects in this book, you will need to do some hemming by hand, as well as sew on buttons and other fastenings or decorations. And when it comes to sustainable sewing, where you want to repair or customise existing garments, basic hand sewing skills are extremely useful.

Hand sewing needles

You will need a variety of hand sewing needles in your sewing kit. Sharps and betweens are the most commonly used ones. Sharps are universal hand sewing needles, whereas the shorter betweens are preferred by quilters and crafters. Slim embroidery needles are great for all kinds of hand sewing, as they have a slightly bigger eye. Avoid very short needles for dressmaking, as they are less practical.

These are the needles most useful for dressmaking:

- Sharps – these are medium-length needles and the most popular for general hand sewing.
- Betweens – these needles are shorter and are useful for quilting.
- Embroidery/crewel needles – these have a longer eye, which makes them very handy for hand sewing with double or quadruple thread, such as fastenings.
- Darning needles – these are generally longer, blunter needles with long eyes, used for darning but also for basting fabrics together.
- Self-threading needle – if you have difficulty threading your hand sewing needle, these ones will be your new friends.

....

TOP TIP

Cut a length of thread, fold it in half and put the two tails through the eye of your needle. This way you can start your stitch without a knot (you sew through the loop of your first stitch instead), so it's much stronger.

....

Thimble

A thimble is essential for hand sewing to protect your hands. Wear the thimble on your middle finger and use it to push the back of the needle through the fabric to get a swift hand sewing motion. You can get thimbles with closed tops or open tops (tailoring style). Which one you pick is down to personal preference.

PRESSING EQUIPMENT

Pressing (as opposed to ironing) is essential at every stage of the dressmaking process in order to achieve a neat, professional-looking finish. Whereas ironing is the process of making a material crease free, pressing is done to ensure that all constructional seams and elements are lying flat throughout the making process, to ensure a neater finish.

Steam iron

A good iron with a steam button is essential for sewing: pressing in between each step, and getting crisp seams and darts, will give your makes a professional finish. Always test a swatch of your fabric with the iron to make sure you have the correct heat setting. If in doubt, use a pressing cloth – a piece of folded cotton in between your iron and your material that protects your fabric from direct contact with the iron. This is particularly good for very lightweight fabrics, laces and silks, as direct contact with the hot iron can distort the delicate fibres.

TOP TIP

Turn off your iron between sewing stages in order to save energy.

Tailor's ham

Pressing your garment on a tailor's ham makes it easier to press open curved seams such as sleeves, collars, armholes, French seams and waistbands.

There's a tutorial on how to make your very own tailor's ham using fabric scraps on page 100.

THREAD

Use a good-quality thread while sewing, as poor-quality thread has a tendency to snap when used on a sewing machine. Remember that an overlocker requires finer thread than a sewing machine, whereas overlocker thread on a sewing machine is far too thin.

You can chose from polyester, silk, cotton, organic cotton and recycled thread made from 100% recycled plastic bottles. As a rule, polyester thread is stronger, so we fully recommend you try the recycled polyester threads. You can match the thread type to the fibre used in your fabric, such as cotton thread for a cotton fabric, but as a general rule of thumb you should match the thickness of your thread to the thickness of your fabric's fibres. As an example, lightweight silk is made of very fine fibres and polyester is actually the finest thread. Silk thread would be too thick on lightweight silk and would interrupt the fibres too much to be able to pass through.

TOP TIP

When looking for a thread to match your fabric colour, unwind some of the thread and lay it on top of the fabric to double check the match, as the thread looks more intense in colour when it's wrapped on the spool.

OTHER USEFUL EQUIPMENT

Below are some other useful accessories for your sewing kit that don't fit into a particular category. The unpicker will be particularly useful, regardless of your sewing experience: we all make mistakes and even the most experienced maker will need one of these close by.

Bamboo pointer

This amazing tool is used for creating crisp corners when you turn pieces such as collars or cuffs inside out. Really old-fashioned ones were made of bone and most modern ones are made of wood. These are great to use, as the point is blunt: using a pencil or small scissors will potentially poke a hole.

Pattern paper/tracing paper

These are required for tracing the PDF patterns included with the book and for creating your own sewing patterns. You can choose from the classic dot-and-cross and gridded pattern papers, which help place the pattern on the grain of the fabric, or a plain tracing paper, which is easier to see through.

Quick unpick

A quick unpick, also called a seam ripper or an unpicker, is a small claw-like tool used to unpick stitching as well as to open buttonholes.

Getting started

This chapter sets out a few tips for you on how to get started and some guides to techniques that will be referred back to in the project instructions. There are different ways of pretreating your fabric and marking it out , depending on what kind of material you have chosen. This chapter will also show you some tips for pattern matching and give you a guide to inserting regular and invisible zips and stitching curved seams and French seams.

Pretreating your fabric

When you decide on a fabric and have picked an exciting new project, it's hard to resist the temptation to start on your sewing project straightaway, but spending a little time preparing your fabric first will pay off in the long run. Here are some useful tips on what you should do before getting started:

PREWASHING

- Most fabrics have some amount of shrinkage, cotton typically having the highest percentage of shrinkage. If you want to test how much your fabric will shrink, see page 23. Always wash your fabric before you start sewing a garment, so that the fabric has shrunk before you start your project. It can be really frustrating if you forget to wash your fabric and your newly made garment shrinks after the first wash.

- Prewashing is also a way to get rid of any coating that might be on the fabric if the fabric has been dyed or printed. A fabric can feel much stiffer when you buy it than after its first wash.

- If you have washed a fabric made from synthetic fibres and the fibres have shrunk in unequal amounts, you will have to try and steam iron this back into shape to correct the grain. See page 43 for more information on mixed fibres.

- Fabrics made from purely synthetic fibres typically shrink much less than fabrics made from natural fibres. After the initial wash, the fabric should have shrunk to its maximum capacity and it won't shrink again.

- You don't have to wash wool before you start, but you should steam it. Use the steam function on your iron and press down onto the wool. Then lift your iron up and move to the next spot. It's important to lift the iron and not drag it across the fabric as this will pull the fabric off grain: wool is very suitable for manipulation, which is how you can steam in beautiful shapes around the collar on a tailored garment, but it also means you have to be careful not to distort the weave when handling it.

PRESSING

- After you've prewashed your fabric, it's a good idea to press it once it's dry before you cut out your pieces. Fabrics like cotton and linen like a hot iron, whereas silk needs a much cooler setting to avoid wrinkling. Remember that fabrics with synthetic fibres essentially contain plastic and plastic melts when it's exposed to high temperatures; so too can your fabric! Press these materials on a cooler setting than you would cottons.

- Metallic threads tend to shrink a lot so be sure to give metallic fabrics a good press before you start.
- Be careful with fabric that has lace inserts when ironing, as lace can easily melt.
- Also think about pretreating any trims you might apply to your garment. If you are applying a metallic braid onto your garment, follow the tip opposite on steaming wool and steam press the braid to make sure it shrinks before you apply it. If you sew a trim or a braid to a garment and the trim or braid shrinks in the wash, it will wrinkle up the fabric around it – and once this has happened, there's nothing you can do about it.

Working with directional prints

Fabrics with a print can either be directional or non-directional. A non-directional print is easy to work with, as it means the print works in all directions and doesn't have an obvious up or down.

NON-DIRECTIONAL PRINT

DIRECTIONAL PRINT

Examples of a non-directional print include an all-over polka-dot print or a stripe. A non-directional print means that you can cut your pattern pieces out with the print going up or going down, because it won't make a difference.

A directional print, on the other hand, means there is a definitive up and down to the print, even though it might not always be obvious straight away. This means that you have to decide which way you want the print to go on your garment and then make sure you follow this direction on all your pattern pieces. For example, you will want to avoid cutting one trouser leg with the print going up and one with the print going down. If the fabric has a very busy print and you can't immediately work out whether it has a direction or not, try to focus on one element of the print, find the repeating pattern and then decide whether it has a direction.

Some fabrics don't have a print but are still directional. One example is velvet, which has a nap – the direction the little hairs on the velvet go. If you stroke it one way it will feel soft and smooth; stroke it the other way and it will feel rougher. The nap on velvet also captures light differently, so it's very important to cut all your pattern pieces with the nap going in the same direction. For dressmaking we generally have the nap going down the body: imagine running your hand downwards over a skirt and that's the direction that should feel the softest.

A shot silk (also called taffeta), which is woven with warp and weft threads in different colours, can look entirely different in colour depending on which direction you look at it. For these fabrics it's also important to cut the pattern pieces in the same direction. It can help to write 'Up' and 'Down' on the edges of your fabric, so that you don't forget when you lay out your pieces.

With a directional print or one with a nap, it's generally best to cut your pieces from a single layer of fabric. This also makes it easier to pattern match (see page 22).

Pattern matching

Pattern matching means ensuring that a fabric print runs continuously across seams. If you have a very small, all-over print you don't need to worry about this, but if you are working with a big print, a big stripe or a check, it can be really satisfying to pattern match across your seams.

Pattern matching sometimes takes up more fabric, as you will need to space your pattern pieces out to capture a certain part of the print. If you have a very big print you can also think about the positioning of the print on your garment: if you have a big floral design on a plain background, for example, it would be a shame to end up with a garment where the flower is slightly off centre or is cut off by a side seam.

TIPS FOR PATTERN MATCHING

1   Cut out your pattern pieces in single layers instead of double, so that you can match them to each other. With a fabric that is placed on the fold, you won't be able to see what's going on on the reverse.

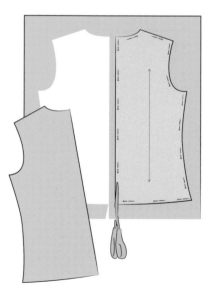

2   If you need to pattern match a small piece, such as a pocket on a coat, position the paper pattern piece on top of the material where the pocket will sit and draw the print onto your paper. Remove your paper and pin it onto the fabric that you're cutting the pocket from, matching the print lines, so that the print aligns.

Pinning, marking and cutting

There are a few different ways to pin, mark and cut out your pattern pieces and the different methods depend on your fabric choice and personal preference.

PINNING

Choose between pinning your pattern pieces to the fabric or weighing them down with pattern weights. Pins will leave marks in very delicate fabrics, so weights might be a better choice; alternatively, you could use special silk pins. For more tips on how to handle delicate fabrics, see page 61.

The grain line on your pattern piece should always be parallel to the selvedge, so that the grain line of the fabric runs lengthwise on the body. If you are sewing a homeware project and your fabric has the same warp and weft threads (100% cotton, for example) with no direction to it, you could cut on the cross grain if you have to. However, we don't recommend using the cross grain for dressmaking. You can find the straight of grain by finding the selvedge of your fabric: this is the very edges of the woven fabric and indicates the end of the weave. You can usually recognise it by looking for the edge that has a finished look, or look for a row of small puncture marks, the name of your fabric or an unprinted or white edge of a fabric that has been dyed or printed. On a fabric with no stretch, the straight of grain and cross grain don't stretch; only the diagonal grain, called the bias, has a stretch.

MARKING OUT YOUR PATTERN PIECES

Before you remove the pattern pieces from your fabric, you will need to transfer markings such as darts and buttonhole positions.

Tailor's chalk

You can use fabric chalk and chalk around the outline of the pattern piece if you need to add seam allowances to a pattern. The patterns that come with this book come with the seam allowance included, so you only need to cut around the pattern piece. However if you are adding more space or lengthening a hem, you will find you need to use something to mark it with, and of course for transferring your pattern markings. The type of chalk used for dressmaking is known as tailor's chalk and comes in different colours.

Air- or water-soluble marker

You can use an air- or water-soluble marker. A water-soluble marker will disappear after a wash, whereas an air-soluble marker reacts with oxygen and simply disappears after a while. It's worth testing these markers on a scrap of your chosen fabric before you feel tempted to scribble all over your project.

Dressmaker's carbon paper

Select a colour of carbon paper that will show up on your fabric and slide it underneath your fabric so that the coloured (carbon) side of the paper is facing the wrong side of the fabric. Run the tracing wheel around the outline of the pattern; this will produce a line of coloured dots on the wrong side of the fabric.

There are different types of tracing wheels with either long spikes or short spikes, and you can also get wheels without spikes that look like a mini rotary cutter. Use the spiky wheels without carbon paper to mark out really fine fabrics: you will end up with a line of small dots, which eliminates the need for a coloured line.

··

TOP TIP

Fold your carbon paper in half so that you have the coloured side on both sides, then slot it in between two layers of fabric. Use your tracing wheel as per usual and mark two lines at the same time.

··

Tacking

For patterns that you need to add seam allowances to, you can also tack around a pattern piece either by hand or by machine as an alternative to marking it with chalk or pen. Hand tacking a pattern piece or tacking in pattern lines such as darts is very common in tailoring, as wool won't mark clearly with other techniques due to its slightly fluffy fibre. Hand tacking is done with a single thread and no knots, so that you can easily pull it out when your garment is finished. You can also machine tack by using the biggest stitch on your machine and tacking around the pattern piece.

Tailor's tacks

For woollen and sheer fabrics, chalk marks are likely to fall off the surface. If you need to transfer dots and circle marks (see page 12) from the pattern to the fabric, traditional tailor's tacks are the best option.

1 Thread a needle with a double thread, but do not knot the end. Make a stitch through the circle mark on the pattern, taking it through both layers of fabric and leaving a 2.5-cm (1-in.) tail.

2 Make a second stitch in the same place, so that you've sewn a loop. Cut the thread, leaving another 2.5-cm (1-in.) tail.

3 Gently prise the two layers of fabric apart and cut the threads in the middle. You now have thread on either side of your pieces.

CUTTING

To cut out your pieces after everything is marked up, you can use either dressmaking shears or a rotary cutter with a cutting mat. Rotary cutters are great for stretch materials and very fine materials. Make sure you maintain the blades on both scissors and rotary cutters for accurate results. Use your scissors or small snips to cut the pattern notches.

....

TOP TIP

Make sure you don't hit a pin when you're cutting, as this will cause a dent in the scissor blade that no amount of sharpening will get rid off.

....

Useful sewing techniques

Here's a brief reminder of some standard dressmaking techniques that you will encounter time and time again.

....

COMMON HAND STITCHES

Slipstitch A stitch commonly used to finish garments or projects in an invisible way. Insert the needle into the fold of the hem, between the two layers of fabric. Pick up the smallest amount of fabric (just a few threads) above the fold and travel along the fold before bringing the needle out and picking up threads to make the next stitch.

Herringbone stitch Another stitch commonly used on hems. Pick up the smallest amount of fabric from the hem and the fabric above, in a zigzag pattern.

....

SEWING CURVED SEAMS

Here are our top tips for sewing curved seams, such as a princess seam on a bodice.

1 Staystitch any curves before you start your seam, so that they don't stretch out of shape. Typical areas that require staystitching are curved bust seams, necklines and raglan sleeves. Staystitching is done within the seam allowance and is not removed after construction. If the curve is extreme, you may have to snip into the seam allowance up to the staystitch, but try to avoid this as much as you can.

2 Pin the two curves together. One curve will be convex (outward) and one curve will be concave (inward). You can only pin convex to concave, and not the other way around. If you are struggling to get the curve under control, you are probably pinning it the wrong way round. Be sure to pin any balance marks or notches first and distribute your pins evenly. You will find that it's very difficult to pin with the pins parallel to the curved line, so try pinning at a 90-degree angle to the seam line instead. For very extreme curves you will sometimes have to snip into the seam allowance to be able to manoeuvre around the curves.

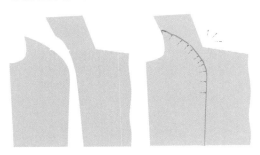

3 Reduce your stitch length slightly to 2.5 to achieve a smooth curved line, then stitch your seam from top to bottom.

4 Finish your seam allowance fairly short on the inside of your garment, so that the seam allowance doesn't buckle and wrinkle under the garment. You can trim the seam allowances and then press them open without finishing them off if you are lining a garment, or overlock the seam allowances together at a foot's width (see Top Tip, page 26) and press them towards the side seam.

FINISHING SEAMS

There are many different ways of finishing your seams; here are the most common.

Overlocking

Overlocking is the quickest and perhaps most common way of finishing seams and requires a separate machine with three or four threads. Domestic overlockers come with the option of threading them with three or four threads, whereas an industrial overlocker comes as either a three-thread or four-thread machine. When using three threads, an overlocker uses only one needle; with four threads, the machine uses two needles. A three-thread overlocker is perfect for all general use, whereas a four-thread overlocker is recommended for stretch fabrics. The double needle makes a double stitch line, which makes it extra strong and therefore suitable for garments that need to stretch.

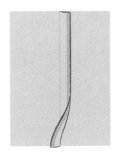

THREE-THREAD OVERLOCK

FOUR-THREAD OVERLOCK

You don't even have to sew your seam first when using a four-thread overlocker: you can overlock your pieces together straightaway and the double stitch line will act as the seam line. Make sure to maintain your overlocker well and remember to use finer threads than on your sewing machine.

Once you're a confident maker, it's good to evaluate where it's appropriate to use an overlocker and where it isn't. An overlocked edge is bulkier, so use your knowledge to establish whether it would be better to finish the seam off in a different way.

Regularly clean out your overlocker to get rid of all the fluff. This fluff clogs up the machine parts and makes the overlocker's performance deteriorate. You will also need to change the blade that trims the fabric every once in a while, as it gets blunt and your results won't be as neat. Follow your machine's instructions on how to do this. If you need to order extra blades, make sure you order the blades that go with your brand of overlocker.

TOP TIP

In this book, we often refer to overlocking 'at a foot's width', which means you end up with a small, neat overlocked seam allowance. To do this, line up the overlocker foot against the seam, so that the blade will trim the seam allowance a foot's width distance away from the seam.

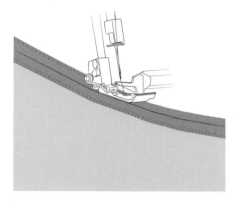

Zigzagging

If you don't have an overlocker, you can always use the zigzag stitch on your sewing machine to finish off a raw edge. This doesn't produce the same effect, but it's the same principle: threads wrap around the raw edge to prevent it from fraying. The best method is to select a fairly wide stitch with a shorter length, to cover more of the raw edge. Position the raw edge under your machine so that the needle drops just off the raw edge before travelling to the other side. Dropping the needle off the edge is essential to this technique. Zigzagging was used until fairly recently as the principal method of finishing raw seam edges, so if you have a look at some vintage garments you will see lots of zigzagged seams.

One of the best ways to use zigzagging is on very lightweight materials like chiffon and organza. Zigzagging over the edge fully draws up the edge because these materials are so lightweight. It creates a finished look with a slightly raised edge. This is how we recommend hemming these fabrics, whether you are hemming a skirt with a sheer top layer or a floaty, chiffon sleeve.

Zigzagging an open seam When you have an open seam, zigzag both sides of the seam allowance separately.

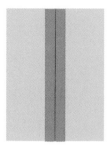

Zigzagging a closed seam For a closed seam, zigzag the two sides together as one layer.

French seam

A French seam is a great way to finish sheer or fine fabrics. For the guide below, we are assuming your pattern has a 1.5-cm (⅝-in.) seam allowance.

1 Place your garment pieces wrong sides together and stitch your first seam line, using a 1-cm (⅜-in.) seam allowance. Counterintuitively, your seam allowances should now be visible on the outside of your garment. Trim the seam allowance to about 3 mm (⅛ in.).

2 Fold the garment pieces so they're right sides together, with the seam right on the fold, and press. Try to be really precise so that the stitch line ends up right on the pressed fold. Position the seam under your presser foot, with the edge of the foot against the folded edge. Stitch a second stitch line a foot's width (5 mm/¼ in.) away from the fold to encase the raw edges.

COMMON MACHINE STITCHING TECHNIQUES

Staystitching A stitch on a curved pattern piece that prevents the fabric from stretching. Stay stitching is done within the seam allowance, so it will never be visible in the finished garment.

Understitching Use this stitch with a facing or a lining to encourage the facing or lining to sit inside the garment. Press all the seam allowances towards the facing, then with the facing right side up under your machine, stitch a line a few millimetres into the facing. You can use your machine foot as a guide.

Topstitching This is a visible stitch done on the outside of a garment to reinforce or decorate a stitch. It's usually done a few millimetres away from the seam and with a slightly bigger stitch length. It's very common on denim, pockets and coats and you can buy special, heavier topstitching thread if you like.

INSERTING A STANDARD ZIP

The method below is a foolproof way of inserting a regular zip and you can have fun with topstitching when you feel really confident with your stitching to make a feature of your zip.

Make sure you overlock or zigzag stitch the seam allowances before you start on the zip and we always recommend testing your zip before you insert it to make sure it works. You need a regular zip foot for this kind of zip.

1 Machine tack together the seam of the garment where you are intending to insert the zip. For a garment that has a zip inserted partly into a seam, like a dress or a skirt, sew up the seam from the hem to the zip notch on a normal stitch length, backstitch, then machine tack the rest of the seam. Press the seam allowances open.

2 With the wrong side of the garment facing you, place the zip face down on the seam. Pin it in place so that the zip teeth lie in the middle of the seam, inserting the pins horizontally. If you need a fastening above the zip, like a hook and bar on a dress, or if a waistband is going to be attached, make sure the zip head lies 1.5 cm (⅝ in.) below the raw edge.

3 Turn the garment right side up and pin the zip in place, pinning around it in a big U-shape in the direction you're going to sew it. This depends on your machine's zipper foot and the brand of your machine: you want the foot to sit next to the zip so that you can stitch fairly close to it. On some machines the zip foot is static and you change the needle position; on other, you unclip the foot and can position it to the left or the right of the needle. Indicate where you want to cross over the bottom of the zip to sew the other side. Mark this with a pin just above the metal or plastic stopper of the zip, so you don't break your needle!

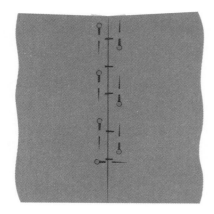

4 Remove the pins from the wrong side of the zip and start stitching from the top. Pivot and stitch across the bottom, then pivot again and continue stitching on the other side.

5 Unpick the tacking stitches from step 1: your zip should now sit beautifully in the centre of the seam.

INSERTING AN INVISIBLE ZIP

An invisible zip doesn't have to be scary and the process is made a lot easier by using an invisible zip foot. Invisible zips visually look different from regular zips as the teeth are not exposed, but are slightly curled under. This is why you need to use a different foot to get as close to the teeth as possible.

Insert an invisible zip before you do the rest of the seam if possible. If you have a waist seam in the middle of your zip, start at step 1; if not, start at step 2.

··

TOP TIP

The only part of an invisible zip that you will see in your finished garment is the puller. A great tip to make the puller blend in entirely is to paint it with nail varnish.

··

1 Position the zip tape along the centre back of the garment and make a pen mark where it matches the waist seam. The top edge of the zip tape (not the top of the functional part of the zip) should reach the top of your garment. Make a mark on each side of the zip tape.

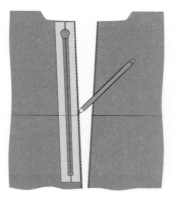

2 Unzip your zip and iron the teeth slightly away from the tape to make it easier to attach. Use a cool setting or the zip will melt. You can sometimes get away without this step but it can make things easier if you are new to this method.

3 With the right side of the garment facing you, lay the right-hand side of the zip tape right side down on the left-hand side of the garment opening. Pin in place, matching the mark you made earlier with the waist seam (if this applies to your garment). If you are nervous about the zip moving while you sew, you can tack the zip in place at this point either by hand or by machine.

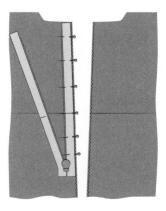

4 Start stitching from the top by slotting the zip teeth into the left groove of the invisible zipper foot. Sew as far down as you can; you will have to stop when you reach the zip pull.

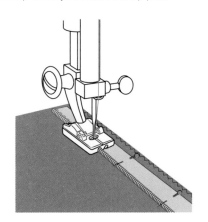

5 Now position and pin the other side of the zip to the remaining side of your garment opening. Be careful not to get the zip twisted.

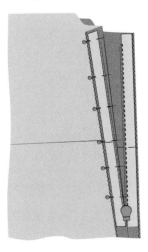

6 Sew from the top down by slotting the zip teeth into the right groove of the invisible zipper foot.

7 Test your zip and give your garment a gentle press.

8 Close the zip. Pin the rest of the seam right sides together and stitch with a regular zip foot. You will have to start a little bit above and away from your zip stitch line to avoid the bulk of the zip pull. Also pull out the end of the zip tape so it's not in the way.

PRACTICE MAKES PERFECT

And finally we want to encourage you to play, try different methods and fail, so that you can learn what you prefer, what works best and improve your skills little by little. Practice makes perfect, and in sewing there are many different ways to achieve the same result. It's one of those wonderful pastimes where you are never done learning. There will always be a technique you have never tried or a method that someone passes on to you to make something easier. Don't feel disheartened that there isn't a straightforward, 'right' way to do every sewing process; instead, feel encouraged that there are many ways to achieve the same thing and you get to pick the one you prefer.

Sizing

The beauty of sewing your own clothes is that you can make clothes that actually fit, instead of having to try to fit into standardised sizes. This chapter sets out everything you need to know to make pattern adjustments to fit your own body shape and size.

Differences in sizes

Don't take it as a bad thing if you have to make pattern adjustments: see it as an opportunity to achieve a great fit that you would never be able to get with shop-bought garments. We all have our quirks and being able to apply them to your patterns takes a bit of practice, but the results will be worth it.

Every pattern and fashion company has its own size chart, as there is no longer a universal size chart based on real people's actual body measurements: the last sizing census was in the 1950s, so companies have been winging it ever since.

Home sewing patterns are usually drafted for women who are about 1.65–1.70 m (5ft 5 in.–5 ft 7 in.) tall with a B cup bust, while men's patterns are generally based on a height of 1.73–1.80 m (5 ft 8 in.–5 ft 11 in.). This is to be able to have a starting point from which makers can adapt their patterns to fit, as that particular height and/or cup size is only applicable to a small proportion of the population (as with all standardised or generic measurements). Once you know your actual size, you can adjust your patterns accordingly to get a perfect fit.

HOW TO MEASURE YOURSELF

Wear your normal underwear when you measure yourself, as that's what you will be wearing underneath any clothing you make; don't measure yourself over your clothes. Measure your height barefoot against a wall.

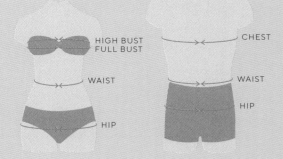

Full bust/chest

Measure across the fullest part of your bust, usually at nipple height. For men, make sure the tape measure lies just underneath the armpit to get the widest part of the chest.

Waist

This is the part of your torso just underneath your lowest rib. If you bend to the side, your waist is where your skin creases under your ribs.

Hip

Your hip is the widest part of your bum and upper thighs. Measure with your feet together. The measurement around your hip bones is called high hip.

High bust

Wrap a tape measure above your bust line, high under your armpits. The difference between your full bust and high bust indicates whether you need to do a full or small bust adjustment (see page 35).

Inside leg

Measure the inside of your leg by holding a tape measure as high up on your inner thigh as you can and ask someone to check the length where the tape measure hits the floor. Make sure you stand up straight or else the measurement will come up shorter.

Nape to waist

Have someone measure you along your spine from your top vertebra to your waist. We all have different-length torsos and if you have a very long or very short torso, you will probably have to adapt your pattern to suit.

SIZE CHARTS IN CM/INCHES FOR MEN AND WOMEN FOR THIS BOOK

The size charts in this book are based on a height of 1.65–1.7 m (5 ft 5 in.–5 ft 7 in.) and a B cup for women and a height of 1.73–1.8 m (5 ft 8 in.–5 ft 11 in.) for men.

Women	4	6	8	10	12	14	16	18
Bust (cm)	83	88	93	98	103	108	113	118
Bust (in.)	32½	34½	36½	38½	40½	42½	44½	46½
Waist (cm)	64	69	74	79	84	89	94	99
Waist (in.)	25	27	29	31	33	35	37	39
Hip (cm)	90	95	100	105	110	115	120	125
Hip (in.)	35½	37½	39½	41½	43½	45¼	47¼	49¼

Men	34	36	38	40	42	44
Chest (cm)	86	91	96	101	106	111
Chest (in.)	33¾	35¾	37¾	39¾	41¾	43¾
Waist (cm)	74	79	84	89	94	99
Waist (in.)	29	31	33	35	37	39
Hip (cm)	91.5	96.5	101.5	106.5	111.5	116.5
Hip (in.)	36	38	40	42	44	46

GRADING IN BETWEEN SIZES

The beauty of having all pattern sizes on the same pattern sheet is that you can easily grade in between the different sizes to suit your measurements. If you are a size 16 on the bust and waist but a size 18 on the hips, for example, you can draw in a smooth line from 16 to 18 in between the waist and the hip to achieve a more personal pattern. You can use a pattern master or a French curve for this to get a really smooth line. It's a great idea to do this in a colour so you can see where to cut when you have finished grading.

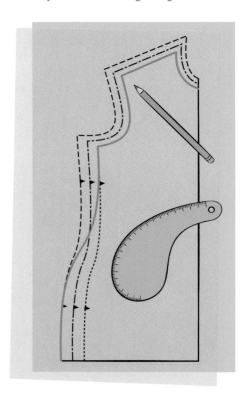

Another way to easily add a bit more space into a pattern is to add to the centre back if you have a seam there. The centre back seam is a straight line, so this way you can easily add up to 2.5 cm (1 in.) without having to redraw side seams, which will typically have some shaping to them.

ALTERING THE LENGTH

Sometimes you need more or less length in a pattern – for example, because your upper body is tall/short or because you have long/short legs. You can determine whether you need more or less length in a bodice by taking your nape-to-waist measurement and comparing that to the pattern. Some patterns have a line that indicates where you can shorten and lengthen, which is positioned in such a way that it doesn't interfere with things like darts. If you don't see a line on your pattern, you can always add or remove length at the bottom of a pattern if it's a question of a longer or shorter hem, or draw a horizontal line across the pattern. If you are lengthening or shortening by more than 2.5 cm (1 in.), you may want to do it in two different places so as not to disturb the design of the pattern too much.

Lengthening

Cut your pattern across the lengthen/shorten line and spread the pattern pieces apart by the amount that you need. If you are adding length in two different places and you want to add 5 cm (2 in.) in total, spread by 2.5 cm (1 in.) in each area. Slide a piece of paper behind and stick your new pattern down with tape. Then use a ruler or a French curve to smooth out the outlines of your new pattern. This is called trueing.

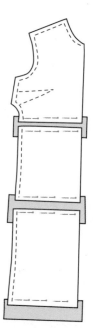

Shortening

Fold the pattern across the lengthen/shorten line or draw a horizontal line across the pattern. Then make a tuck that's half the amount you want to shorten by: if you want to shorten by 3 cm (1¼ in.), for example, make a 1.5-cm (⅝-in.) tuck. Use tape to stick down the tucks and redraw any outside lines that need smoothing out.

ALTERING WAIST DARTS

An easy way to adapt patterns that have waist darts is to take in the darts a bit more or less than the pattern requires. This is suitable for small pattern alterations to the waist. Divide the alteration between the number of darts – so if you want to take in the waist by 2 cm (¾ in.) and you have four darts, make each dart 5 mm (³⁄₁₆ in.) more than the pattern. The same goes for adding space to the waist: reduce the darts slightly to make the waist a bit bigger.

TROUSER ADJUSTMENTS

There are two common adjustments you can easily make to trouser patterns: the crotch depth and the crotch length.

Adjusting crotch depth

Crotch depth is the measurement between your waist and crotch line. You can measure this by sitting on a chair and measuring from your natural waist to the surface of the chair. This measurement is what determines the rise in a pair of trousers and is very different on each person.

To shorten or lengthen the crotch depth on your pattern, use the same process as described on the left for shortening and lengthening in general. Cut along the hip line on your trouser pattern, then spread to increase or fold to reduce. Make sure you true any pattern edges before proceeding. If there is no hip line on your pattern, draw a horizontal line by estimating: your hipline lies 18–23 cm (7–9 in.) below your natural waist.

Adjusting crotch length

Crotch length is the measurement taken from the front waist, through your legs, to your back waist. This measurement differs widely from one person to another and has a lot to do with your body shape.

1 Measure yourself, then measure the crotch curve on the pattern. Divide the difference in half, which is the measurement you will use to spread or reduce the curve by.

2 Mark a horizontal line 8 cm (3 in.) below the trouser waist on both your front and back trouser pattern. Cut along this line and leave a hinge at the side seam.

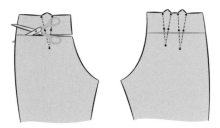

To increase crotch length

Spread the pattern by the amount you calculated in step 1, leaving the side seam as it is. Slide some paper behind and stick your new pattern down with tape. Smooth out the crotch curve.

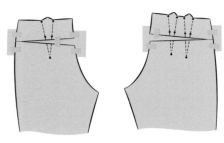

To reduce crotch length

Overlap the pattern by the amount you calculated in step 1, leaving the side seam as it is. Tape it in place and smooth out the crotch curve.

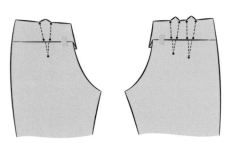

TOP TIP

If you have a round bum, you might need extra space in the back crotch only. Use this technique to spread the crotch curve on your back trouser pattern only. The same goes for a flatter bum: reduce the crotch curve on the back trouser pattern only.

BUST ADJUSTMENTS

You may need to alter the fit at the bust in three ways: to accommodate for a small or full bust, or to move the bust point on the bust dart. The bust point is the fullest point of your bust, which can sit higher or lower on each woman. Measure your own bust point from the shoulder down and compare it to the pattern.

Moving a bust dart

1 With a ruler, draw a rectangular box around the bust dart. Cut around the box and move it up or down, keeping the edges of the rectangle parallel to the original position.

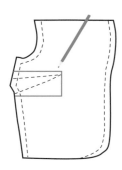

2 Tape the box to its new position and slide a piece of paper behind the pattern to fill the gap. Use a ruler and perhaps a French curve to match up and redraw the outline of your new pattern.

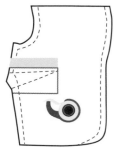

Full or small bust adjustment

Most commercial patterns are cut to fit a B cup, which means some of us will have to adapt our patterns to fit our bust measurements. This can seem more daunting than it is and it will make a big difference to how your clothes fit. The advantage of sewing a garment from scratch is that you can make these adjustments early on and create a garment that will fit much better than a shop-bought item.

If your full bust measurement is bigger than your high bust measurement by more than 6.5 cm (2½ in.), you will need to do a full bust adjustment (FBA). If this is the case, use your high bust measurement as your bust size to determine which pattern size to cut from the size chart. If the difference between your high and full bust is much smaller than 6.5 cm (2½ in.), you may need a small bust adjustment (SBA).

The process for doing a full or small bust adjustment is the same, except that you are either adding space by spreading the pattern or reducing space by overlapping the pattern.

Think about the kind of garment you are making before you adjust your pattern. These adjustments are great for garments with fitted bodices, but are not strictly necessary for floaty garments with lots of ease.

	Example 1: FBA	Example 1: SBA	My Measurements
Full bust measurement	97 cm (38 in.)	89 cm (35 in.)	
High bust measurement	89 cm (35 in.)	86.5 cm (34 in.)	
Difference	8 cm (3 in.)	2.5 cm (1 in.)	
FBA = half the difference	4 cm (1½ in.)		
SBA = half the difference		1.25 cm (½ in.)	

Full bust adjustment

1 Measure from your shoulder to your bust point, then measure the same on your paper pattern to get the position of the bust point. With a ruler, draw a straight line from this point to the hem (make it parallel to the grain line to make sure it's straight). Draw another line from the bust point mark towards the armhole, hitting the lower third of the armhole, or the armhole notch if there is one. This is Line 1. Draw a final line horizontally through the bust dart, meeting Line 1 at the marked bust point. This is Line 2.

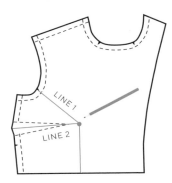

2 Cut along Line 1 from the hem to the armhole, leaving it attached by a small hinge at the armhole so that you can pivot the pattern. Cut along Line 2 as well, leaving a small hinge at the tip of the dart.

3 Line up the cut edges of Line 1 so they have been spread by the amount you need for your FBA. The vertical edges should be parallel to each other, and you will notice that the dart automatically spreads as you do this. The hem is now no longer a nice straight line, so we need to adjust that. Draw a horizontal line parallel to the hem edge, cut along it and move this small piece until the hem edges are even. Slide some paper behind your new pattern and stick your pattern down with tape.

. . . .

TOP TIP

If your bodice pattern is sewn onto another pattern piece, like a skirt, make sure you accommodate for the fact that your bodice pattern is now slightly wider.

. . . .

Small bust adjustment

1 Draw in all the lines as for a FBA. It's the same process, but in reverse.

2 Overlap the darted side of the pattern across the other side by the amount you need for your SBA.

3 Make the same adjustment as above for the FBA to level the hem.

SLASH AND SPREAD

A great method to hack a pattern is to use a technique called slash and spread. With this easy method you can turn a fitted shape into a flared shape: a straight sleeve can become a bell sleeve, an A-line skirt can turn into a more flared skirt, a straight trouser leg can turn into a flared leg.

We will demonstrate this on a sleeve pattern, but once you give it a go you can experiment!

1 Draw vertical lines across your sleeve pattern and cut along these lines, leaving a hinge at the sleeve head. If you draw all the way up to the sleeve head you will get a sleeve that is flared all the way from the top of the sleeve. If you would like a bishop sleeve, you can draw a horizontal line first where you want the volume to start, and then draw vertical lines up to meet this line.

2 You can now spread the different sections by equal amounts, but leaving the sleeve head the same. This means nothing changes in your armhole.

3 Slide pattern paper behind your new pattern and stick your pattern down with tape. Make sure to smooth out the hem.

The variations to this are pretty much endless. You can gather your new sleeve into a cuff if you like, or reverse this hack by slashing and spreading into the sleeve head to create a gathered sleeve head.

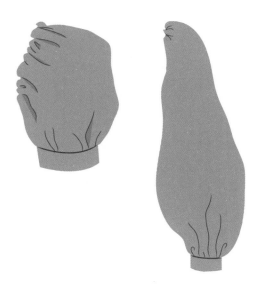

TOILES

If you are new to a pattern or unfamiliar with a particular technique, it can be worth making a toile of the garment or parts of the garment. A toile is a mock-up in a plain fabric such as calico that you can make any adjustments to before cutting into your chosen fabric. If you are making a dress with a fitted bodice and a full skirt, you wouldn't need to toile the skirt but it could be helpful to make a toile of the bodice to get a good fit. If you are making a jacket, you could make a half toile: one half of the front, one half of the back and one sleeve. Toiles are also good if you are struggling to work out a pattern, as they can help you figure out how everything goes together.

Fabrics

Selecting the right fabric is one of the main challenges for home sewers, as choosing the wrong material can jeopardise your make. There are many ways to choose a fabric, from considering the season in which it will be worn to how often you will wear it and what your skill level is. You will find tips throughout the book on how to select a fabric for your garments, introduce you to different types of fabrics and their properties, and finally discuss how to select the appropriate width of fabric for dressmaking.

How to select a fabric

Once you have chosen a pattern to sew, how do you select a fabric to make it in? There are various things to consider, such as the transparency, drape, weight and stretch of a fabric, all of which will determine how suitable a fabric is for the garment you are making. Another way to select fabrics is to look at the fibres that the material has been made from, which can be either natural or synthetic.

WHAT FABRICS DO YOU LIKE?

Many garments can be made in different types of fabrics, depending on the look you are going for, the season it is made for or the garment's intended use; a silk blouse, for example, has a more dressed-up look than a cotton or linen blouse, while a denim skirt looks entirely different to a silk skirt made from the same pattern. Our top tip for selecting a fabric is to go to your wardrobe and see what fabric items are made of. Find a similar garment to the one you are making: what does the fabric feel like? Is it floaty or sturdy? Has it got some body or is it very lightweight? Has it got a shine? Learn what your favourite garments are made of and take it from there.

WHAT'S YOUR SKILL LEVEL?

It's also a good idea to think about your skill level as a maker when selecting a fabric. Typically, woven fabrics such as cottons are recommended for beginners as they behave very well under the machine, they iron nice and flat, and you don't need special tricks to sew a beautiful seam. Stretch fabrics require slightly different tools and techniques, but medium-weight stretch materials are great for all levels of makers. As soon as you get into the territory of very lightweight, very slippery or very transparent fabrics, such as silk and chiffon, you will need a wider repertoire of skills and techniques to create a beautiful garment, as these fabrics don't behave as well. See the top tips on page 61 for working with these types of materials if you are ready to give it a go.

HOW SEE-THROUGH DO YOU WANT THE GARMENT TO BE?

Another good tip is to think about the transparency of fabrics, as this isn't always immediately obvious. Hold the fabric up to the light and see how much light it lets through. If you can see your hand through the fabric and you decide to make a dress out of this material, you will most likely be able to see your legs through the garment in certain lights.

NATURAL OR SYNTHETIC FIBRES?

Another way to select fabrics is to look at the fibres that the material has been made of, which can be either natural fibres, which naturally occur in our environment, or synthetic fibres, which are produced by humans. Natural fibres come from either plants or animals, and they are renewable and biodegradable. Some examples of natural fibres made from animals are wool, mohair, silk and cashmere. Wool comes from sheep, mohair comes from Angora goats, cashmere comes from Cashmere goats, and silk is produced by silk worms.

Examples of fibres derived from plants are cotton, flax (which makes linen), jute, hemp and bamboo. Natural fibres have great properties for dressmaking, such as water absorbency, heat retention and breathability. Natural fibres have been used by humans for thousands of years to produce materials and are less impactful on the planet as well as on our skin. Babies and people with allergies often benefit from wearing natural fibres.

Rayon, also known as viscose, is a tricky fibre to define as it's made from plant cellulose but processed in a chemical way. It's used in garments with drape and very popular in the fashion industry. Rayon/viscose is made by extracting plant cellulose, or the wood pulp, from trees such as beech, pine and eucalyptus, or plants like bamboo, soy and sugarcane. It's then submerged in a chemical solution to produce a substance that can be woven into fibres. It has the potential to become more environmentally friendly by reusing or recovering the chemicals to produce a more closed loop production, instead of letting the chemicals pollute waterways and industry workers, and by using wood pulp from regulated sources.

Synthetic fibres have entirely other properties and are made through chemical processes. The main component in synthetic fibres is oil, which produces plastic fibres. Some common examples of synthetic fibres are polyester, nylon and acrylic. Synthetic fibres are not very breathable, but can be engineered to have properties like being waterproof, moisture wicking or crease free. Nylon is an entirely synthetic fibre made from mainly petroleum oil. It can be used in a woven fabric to add stretch to a fibre like cotton, but has predominantly been used in sportswear, tights and stockings. Spandex, Lycra or elastane are all different names for an entirely synthetic fibre that produces a stretch fibre, which can be added to a woven fabric to produce things like tight sportswear, socks, tights, underwear, form-fitting garments and jeans. Lycra is technically a brand name, whereas elastane or spandex is the name for the fibre. This fibre is so common that we all own something that contains this material, even though it is very detrimental to the environment due to its synthetic properties.

Some other examples of less common synthetic fabrics, but which we have all encountered, are neoprene (made from rubber and used in, for example, wetsuits), scuba (the dressmaking alternative to neoprene and made from polyester and nylon or spandex), power mesh (a mesh used in dance wear and costumes), Lurex (a brand name for a synthetic metallic fibre) and latex (synthetic rubber used in, for example, medical gloves and rain boots).

For tips on how to care for garments made from synthetic fibres, see Laundry & Dry Cleaning on page 156.

Fabric types and their properties

Here we introduce you to woven, non-woven and knit fabrics, the ways different fibres can be combined and how this impacts on the fabric's ability to shrink or stretch.

WOVEN FABRICS

Woven fabrics are woven from warp (vertical) and weft (horizontal) threads and come in lots of different types and weights. Cottons, polyesters, silks, voiles, woollens, chiffons and denims are examples of woven fabrics. These fabrics typically don't have a stretch to them, unless they are woven with a mix of fibres, one of which contains stretch.

Woven fabrics that are used for dressmaking are generally cut with the grain line of the pattern piece parallel to the selvedge of the fabric, as this works with gravity to create a garment that hangs nicely down the body. When cut on the bias, woven fabrics will stretch and this is used to create drape in certain areas of a garment. Woven fabrics can be made in so many different ways and with many different colours to create beautiful patterns. They may also contain metallic thread to add shimmer. Some examples of names of weaves are brocade, damask, satin, jacquard and herringbone, which all refer to a certain way of creating a weave.

KNIT FABRICS

Knit fabrics are mainly stretch fabrics that are made by fibres that loop together like in a knitted garment. Knit fabrics include interlock, which is a fabric that looks the same on both sides and has fine ribs running across the surface; double knit, which also looks the same on both sides but is much sturdier and actually has no stretch to it; and jersey knit, which is a popular knit fabric and is distinguished by having a very clear right side and wrong side. Jersey comes in different mixes of fibres and different amounts of stretch. A stretch fabric that has become very popular with home sewing is ponte, also known as ponte di Roma, which is a type of double knit fabric that is very stable and easy to work with.

Stretch fabrics can have a two-way stretch (the material stretches from selvedge to selvedge only) or a four-way stretch (the material stretches in all directions) and it's best to sew these materials with a ballpoint needle. Two other terms that are useful when discussing stretch materials are stretch retention and recovery. Recovery refers to the ability of the fabric to return to its original size after it has been stretched out. This would be very important in a garment like a leotard. If a material has bad recovery, it means it grows after having been stretched out. This is why your wool knitted cardigans should be dried flat: if they stretch out on the drying rack, they will grow a little bit each time as they have bad recovery. Shape retention refers to how well a fabric will hold its shape over time.

When you buy a fabric that contains stretch, it should indicate – with a percentage – how much it will stretch. Dressmaking patterns that are designed for stretch fabrics take this percentage into consideration and if you are making a form-fitting garment, the pattern will be slightly smaller than your body measurements to account for the stretch.

NON-WOVEN FABRICS

Non-woven fabrics are either felted or bonded together and form an entirely separate category of materials with very unique properties. The most common example of a felted non-woven fabric is wool felt, which can be used in crafting and toys. Other examples of non-woven materials are PVC fabric and fake leather. Interfacing can often be a non-woven material. Non-woven fabrics are not really used for dressmaking and are more often used in industrial ways.

MIXED-FIBRE FABRICS

All woven fabrics are made up of a warp (vertical threads) and a weft (horizontal threads). If these two threads are made of the same fibre, you have a fabric that is 100%: 100% cotton or 100% linen, for example. The warp and weft threads can also be made of different fibres, creating a mixed content: polycotton, for example, is woven with cotton and polyester threads. When selecting a mixed fibre, you are looking at the properties of each fibre. If you would like to use a linen, but you know that 100% linen creases very easily and you want to avoid this, you can select a linen fabric that has been woven with a fibre that doesn't crease so easily. The same thing goes for stretch. If you select a fabric that is 95% cotton and 5% elastane, it has all the great properties of a cotton fabric with the added bonus of having a slight stretch.

SHRINKAGE

It's important to note that nearly all dressmaking fabrics have some shrinkage. This means that after the fabric has been washed for the first time, it will have shrunk by a certain percentage.

You can check this percentage by consulting with the retailer or by testing it yourself. Measure and cut a square, wash it and measure how much it's shrunk in size. As a rule of thumb, cotton shrinks the most, by roughly 3–5%. This is why washing a fabric before starting your garment is so important: you don't want the garment to shrink once it's been made up. A fabric made from mixed fibres can shrink differently in width than in length, as the fibres react differently to the water and temperature. Carefully ironing your fabric after the wash will usually help smooth out any irregularities caused by this difference. You can sometimes notice the difference if you can see the fibres of the weave, and you will see that one fibre has pulled slightly off grain. Use your iron to gently encourage your fabric back into shape.

THE WIDTH OF A FABRIC

Most fabrics come woven in widths between 115 and 150 cm (45 and 60 in.), but the 110-cm (45-in.) widths are in reality not very suitable for dressmaking. This narrower width is often used in quilting cottons and it can be hard to get your pattern pieces out of this width, especially once the fabric has been folded in half. Selecting a width of between 130 and 150 cm (50 and 60 in.) ensures that you can cut most pattern pieces out and you don't have any issues cutting on the fold. You can also choose not to cut on the fold, although this is usually only economical in wider widths.

Sustainable sewing

Sewing and sustainability go hand in hand, and we can make this wonderful hobby kinder to the earth without sacrificing our personal style or creative flair. We can all make more sustainable choices when selecting buttons, zips, thread and (best of all) fabric – and this chapter sets out a few tips and tricks on how to achieve this.

Sustainable fabrics

If you want your fabric choices to be more sustainable, here are some questions to ask yourself:

- Can I trace the origin of this fabric? Look for fabrics that clearly display their place of origin so you know what you're buying.

- Was the crop for this fabric farmed in a regulated or organic way? Low use of pesticides is better for the planet as well as for the workers.

- Did this fabric travel far to reach me? Air miles have a high environmental impact.

- Is this fabric made from natural or synthetic fibres? Natural fibres are a more sustainable choice, as they are biodegradable.

- How impactful is the crop that this fabric was made from? Cotton, for example, has a profound environmental impact due to its high water usage, whereas linen has a much lower water usage.

PRINTED AND DYED FABRICS

When buying fabrics that have been printed or dyed, look for a certification of the chemicals used. This ensures that the production of your fabric didn't harm the people working with it or will not cause harm through the wastewater left over after production. Up to 10% of fabric dyes are washed away in the wastewater during the process, so it's a good idea to look out for these certifications.

Digital printing is different from dyeing in that it prints a design on the surface of the base material, rather than dyeing the fibres by soaking. Digital printing uses very little to no water and is the most environmentally friendly way of achieving printed textiles. The traditional way to print textiles is screen printing, which causes a lot of leftover pigments. A digital printer uses exactly what it needs, leaving hardly any residue.

SUSTAINABLE FABRIC OPTIONS

There are lovely sustainable alternatives available for makers who are interested in learning more about the impact of their fabric choices. Some materials are brand new and others are some of the oldest fabrics known to mankind; see the list on the facing page.

Abaca

This fibre comes from the abaca tree, a relative of the banana tree that doesn't bear fruit. This relatively newly developed fibre is durable, strong and very breathable.

Ahimsa silk

Also called peace silk, this is made by silk worms that have been allowed to mature into butterflies. The process does not harm the insects and takes much longer to make than regular silk.

Bamboo

Bamboo is a very sustainable crop, as it's very hardy against diseases and very fast growing. Select an organic or closed-loop production to ensure the production takes care of the chemical components needed to turn the pulp into fibres.

Hemp

Hemp production uses around 3% of the water that cotton production uses and yields the biggest harvest of all natural fibres.

Hessian

Known as burlap in the US and Canada and as crocus in Jamaica, this fabric is made from jute, a plant fibre that's very strong, versatile and affordable. Growing jute purifies the air and the crop grows very quickly. It's often used to make sturdier fabrics, but can also be combined with other fibres to produce more lightweight versions.

Kapok

Made from the kapok tree, this cellulose fibre is very silky and soft to the touch and is hypoallergenic, making it suitable for bedding. Kapok is blended with other fibres to create a fabric, as it cannot be used on its own. It has traditionally been used as a filling material.

Linen

The fibre that linen is woven from, flax, is a much less thirsty crop than cotton and it grows in Europe, too. If you are based in Europe, this means that the fabric hasn't travelled as far, reducing the air miles between the crop and your doorstep.

Pina

This is made from the leaves of the pineapple plant, which can be turned into a fabric. It can be combined with other fibres to create a very lightweight fabric.

Piñatex

This is an innovative alternative to leather made from pineapple leaves, mostly used in vegan shoes and bags that are made to look like leather.

Ramie

Ramie is a flowering plant in the nettle family. It is similar to cotton and linen in weight and weave, but much more durable as a material and the crop is very sustainable to grow.

Tencel

Also known as Lyocell, Tencel is a cellulose fabric made from the wood pulp of trees. It is produced in an environmentally friendly way and certified closed loop. All resources are used at maximum capacity rather than going to waste, leaving a low ecological impact.

OTHER TIPS

- Fabrics that are typically made from plastic content and shed a lot of microfibres into our waste water systems, such as fleece fabric made from polyester fibres, can also use recycled plastic content to make them more environmentally friendly and re-use resources. This is still not great, but it's a step in the right direction.

- Another option you can consider is deadstock fabric, which means you buy leftover fabrics from the fashion industry or the end of bolts of fabrics that would otherwise go to waste because they are hard to sell.

- Use up the fabric you already have at home and try to resist the temptation to buy new fabrics before you have used your stash.

Sustainable haberdashery

New products are frequently coming on to the market offering sustainable alternatives to haberdashery.

THREAD

Thread is often made out of 100% polyester, but there are now more options to choose from, including organic cotton thread, silk and even thread made from 100% recycled plastic bottles.

The plastic thread cones that your thread is often wrapped on are made of polypropylene (or PP for short) and they can be recycled at dedicated recycling points. Phone ahead to make sure they take them, as not all places do.

BUTTONS

After World War Two plastic buttons became more and more popular, as they were cheap to buy and quick to make. There is a wide variety of alternatives that you can use, including wooden, shell, resin and vintage buttons. We all have a bag of old buttons in our sewing box and you can often find them at car boot sales and in second-hand shops.

Another eco-friendly alternative is the corozo button. Corozo is a 100% natural product similar in consistency to a hard resin. Also, known as tagua, it is often referred to as 'vegetable ivory'. At a microscopic level, corozo is made up of very tightly wound organic fibres, which makes it extremely durable.

ZIPS

Zips tend to be made with plastic and polyester tape, which end up in landfill. A great alternative is to use zips with metal teeth. Not only do they look great and give your dressmaking projects a new flair, they also come in a variety of metals such as gold, silver and brass. Metal zips are often made with cotton tape and 100% organic cotton zips are becoming more readily available. You can also source plastic zips made from recycled materials.

TOILES

Keep old bed sheets and fabrics for making toiles, rather than buying new or cheap fabrics. You can even re-use old toiles for other dressmaking projects or toile making.

Offcuts and scrap fabrics

The sewing community are sharing more ways on how to creatively and economically use up your fabric scraps, which is so inspiring. We have even included a few projects in this book which will use up your fabric scraps, such as making your own tailor's ham (see page 100); for more suggestions, turn to pages 84–85.

Scrap fabrics don't need to be thrown away – they can be used in many ways.

- Fabric remnants can be used to wrap gifts as a reusable wrapping paper.

- You can use jersey and soft cotton scraps to make an eye make-up remover pad. Simply cut them into a circle and overlock the edges and you have a reusable make-up pad that you can wash between uses and they make great gifts.

- Quilting is another creative way to use up fabric scraps. Why not try a hexagon quilt with all your past dressmaking fabrics?

- You could phone your local charity shop and ask if they will take your fabric scraps. A lot of them do, to sell as stuffing for craft projects or to sell to keen quilters. Charity shops, of course, also take unwanted items of clothing. It's worth noting that they can't always sell everything they have been given, due to poor quality. So, we recommend that you only donate items that you know can be sold, as charity shops are forced to sell the rest on, often to countries around the world with poor economies.

- Charity shops also take bolts of fabric, so if you are having a proper clear-out of your fabric stash and you want your fabrics to go to a new home in a charitable way, you could go down this route.

- Donate your fabric remnants and scraps to local schools or colleges.

Final thoughts

At the beginning of this chapter we gave you a few criteria to consider when selecting fabric, and we would like to encourage you to decide which ones are important to you.

There is no perfect, sustainable fabric, so prioritise what matters most to you. If you make something out of a synthetic fibre but you wear it forever, then that's a much better choice than making something out of linen and only wearing it three or four times.

There is no such thing as the perfect material, but thinking about it and making a more educated choice is a great step in the right direction. Use up what you have, wear what you make, and make informed choices about the rest.

The Projects

Pussybow Blouse

This pussybow blouse is a lovely alternative to a plain shirt. It features beautiful bound keyhole openings at the wrists and a back yoke that slightly extends over the front shoulder for a timeless look. The sleeves are gathered into cuffs to add volume around the wrist, to balance out the bow. Style wise you could wear your blouse tied in a front bow, tied at the side or leave it untied for a chic 'undone' look. If you decide to make it in a fine fabric, follow our tips on page 61.

TO MAKE THE PUSSYBOW BLOUSE

Materials

- Sizes 4–10: 2.5m (2¾ yd) fabric 115 cm (45 in.) wide or 1.9m (2 yd) fabric 150 cm (60 in.) wide
- Sizes 12–18: 2.6m (2⅞ yd) fabric 115 cm (45 in.) wide or 2m (2¼ yd) fabric 150 cm (60 in.) wide
- 50 cm (20 in.) interfacing for the button placket
- 7–9 small shirt buttons
- 2 small cuff buttons
- Basic sewing kit (see page 14)

Note If you are using a fine fabric, you will also need a size 60 or 70 needle

Difficulty level

Confident beginners and improvers

Fabric suggestions

Lightweight cottons, bamboo silk, chambray, crepe

Design notes

Use a 1.5-cm (⅝-in.) seam allowance throughout, unless otherwise stated.

Instructions are given for overlocking the seam allowances, but if you don't have an overlocker you can neaten the seam allowances by zigzagging them instead.

Finished measurements	4	6	8	10	12	14	16	18
Front length (cm)	55	55.5	56	56.5	57	58	58.5	59
Front length (in.)	21⅝	21¾	22	22¼	22½	22¾	23	23¼
Back length (cm)	58	58.5	59	59.5	60	61	61.5	62
Back length (in.)	22¾	23	23¼	23½	23⅝	24	24¼	24½
Bust (cm)	90.5	95.5	100.5	105.5	110.5	115.5	120.5	125.5
Bust (in.)	35⅝	37½	39½	41½	43½	45½	47½	49½
Waist (cm)	86.5	91.5	96.5	101.5	106.5	111.5	116.5	121.5
Waist (in.)	34	36	38	40	42	44	46	48
Sleeve length (cm)	58.5	59	59.5	60	60.5	61	61.5	62
Sleeve length (in.)	23	23¼	23½	23⅝	23¾	24	24¼	24½

CUTTING GUIDE

115 cm (45 in.) wide fabric

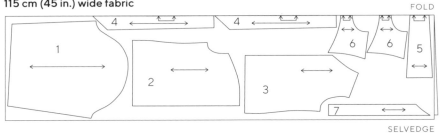
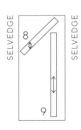

150 cm (60 in.) wide fabric

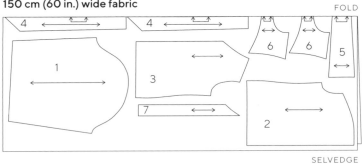
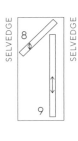

1 Sleeve – cut 2

2 Back blouse – cut 2

3 Front blouse – cut 2

4 Front necktie – cut 2 on the fold

5 Back necktie – cut 1 on the fold

6 Back yoke – cut 2 on the fold

7 Placket – cut 2

8 Keyhole binding – cut 2

9 Cuff binding – cut 1 (makes two)

Notes If you wish, you can apply interfacing to your placket pieces to stabilise them; this is advisable if you are using a fine, slinky fabric such as silk.

If you have a directional print, you will have to cut the back necktie as two pieces, rather than on the fold, and join them with a centre back seam so that the print is mirrored. Add a 1.5-cm (⅝-in.) seam allowance to the pattern piece to achieve this; in step 17, sew the centre back seam and press it open without finishing the seam allowances.

THE SEWING STARTS HERE

1 Construct the back of the blouse
With right sides together, pin and sew the centre back edges of the back blouse together. Press the seam open and overlock the seam allowances separately.

2 Run two lines of gathering stitches across the top of the back blouse, in between the notches. Use the biggest stitch on your machine (don't backstitch) and stitch one line on top of the pattern line and one line a foot's width into the seam allowance.

3 Sandwich the back of the blouse in between the two yokes, with the yokes right sides together. (The yokes will be upside down.) Match the gathering notches on the yoke to the gathering notches on the back of the blouse and then gather up the back of the blouse to fit in between. Put plenty of pins in this are to keep the gathers nice and tidy. Pin along the rest of the seam and sew.

4 Trim the three seam allowances in a staggered way to get rid of any bulk. Press the yoke pieces and all seam allowances upwards, being careful not to press on top of the gathers in the back blouse. Topstitch the yoke seam a foot's width away from the first seam. The two yokes will now be referred to as the outer yoke (visible on the right side of the blouse) and the lining yoke.

5 Construct the front of the blouse
Pin and sew the waist darts in the front of the blouse and press them towards the side seams (see page 118, step 4).

6 Place the back wrong side up. Pin the wrong side of the front blouse to the right side of the lining yoke at the shoulder, pinning through the lining yoke only. Sew and press the seam allowances towards the yoke.

7 Looking at your blouse from the outside, press the shoulder seam of the outer yoke piece under by 1.5 cm (⅝ in.) and lay the pressed-under edge over the front blouse shoulder to trap all raw edges on the inside. Pin and topstitch in place close to the folded edge. Repeat for the other shoulder. You should now have the fronts and back of your blouse lying flat.

8 **Construct the button placket**
Women's garments traditionally fasten right over left (from the wearer's perspective). That means the buttonholes are on the wearer's right and the buttons on the wearer's left. Looking at the inside of your blouse, pin the right side of your placket to the wrong side of the right-hand centre front and stitch in place. Press the long raw edge of the placket under by 1.5 cm (⅝ in.).

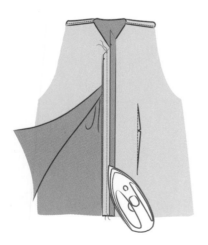

....

TOP TIP

If you are upcycling a shirt, you can re-use an existing button placket (the facing with buttonholes on one side and buttonstand with buttons on the other) to avoid having to make new buttonholes.

....

9 Fold the placket over to the front of the blouse and press, so that the seam is on the centre front edge. Topstitch it in place. Your placket should now measure 3 cm (1¼ in.) in width. Topstitch close to the centre front edge as well. This is where the buttonholes will go.

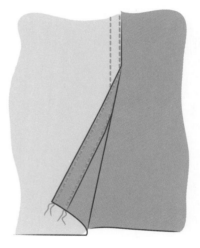

10 Repeat steps 8 and 9 on the other front; this will be the buttonstand – the side to which the buttons are sewn.

11 Construct the sleeves

Run two lines of gathering stitches in between the notches on the sleeve head (as in step 2). With the blouse and sleeve right sides together, match the gathering notches on the sleeve to the gathering notches on the yoke, and match both sleeve points to get the right position, then gather the sleeve head evenly in between those points. Continue pinning the rest of the sleeve head into the armhole. Sew in place, then overlock the seam allowances together at a foot's width and press towards the neck. Repeat for the other sleeve.

TOP TIP

Make sure you pin the correct sleeve into each armhole: the wrist keyhole should be on the back half of your garment.

12 On each long edge of the keyhole binding, press 5 mm (¼ in.) to the wrong side. Then press the binding in half lengthwise, with wrong sides together, making one half a little bit wider than the other. From the right side of the blouse, slot the binding around the raw edge of the keyhole, with the wider edge of the binding on the back. Pin in place and topstitch from the right side. The underneath of the binding is slightly wider, so you will easily catch it.

13 Fold the garment right sides together, matching the underarm and side edges. Pin and sew the underarm and side seams. Overlock the seam allowances together at a foot's width and press towards the back.

14 Run two lines of gathering stitches around the sleeve hem, then gather the hem to 19 cm (7½ in.). Gauge if you need to trim some of the seam allowance down before you attach the binding (depending on the width you are using): the binding folded in half should cover the gathering stitches.

15 Cut the cuff binding piece in half. Press 5 mm (¼ in.) of the binding to the wrong side on each short edge and then each long edge. Then make up the binding, as in step 12. Slot the binding onto the sleeve hem, with the wider edge of the binding on the inside of the garment. Starting from the back of the keyhole opening, pin the binding all the way around the sleeve hem. You should have an excess of about 4 cm (1½ in.), which you will use to make a button loop; trim the binding if necessary.

16 Topstitch the binding in place, starting from the back of the keyhole and stopping 1 cm (⅜ in.) away from the front edge of the keyhole on the other side. Edge stitch through the remainder of the binding and then tuck the end into the binding at the front of the keyhole to create a loop. Topstitch the remaining 1 cm (⅜ in.). Sew a button onto the back of the keyhole binding.

TOP TIP

When looking at a blouse or shirt, a keyhole or cuff should fasten towards the back.

17 Construct the pussybow necktie
With right sides together, pin one front necktie piece to each side of the back necktie piece. Sew the seams and press the seam allowances open. With right sides together, fold the entire tie in half lengthwise and sew the front sections of the tie up to the point where the fronts join the back. Trim the seam allowances of the front sections and turn the tie right side out. Try to get nice sharp corners on the fronts of the tie and press the front sections.

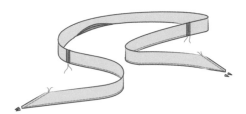

TOP TIP

If you have a directional print, you will have to cut the back neckpiece with a centre back seam rather than on the fold, so that the print is mirrored from the centre back down both fronts of the tie.

18 Press one edge of the back section of the tie under by 1.5 cm (⅝ in.). With right sides together, pin the unpressed edge of the tie to the neckline of the blouse, matching the front of the neckline to the seam in the tie and matching the notch to the shoulder seam. The necktie will be lying upside down on top of the outside of the blouse. Sew, then press the necktie and all seam allowances upwards. Then align the remaining side of the necktie (the one you pressed earlier) to the inside of the neckline and sew from the outside by stitching in the ditch (see page 81, step 12). Alternatively, slipstitch the necktie in place from the inside.

19 Finish the blouse
Turn up a double 1.5-cm (⅝-in.) hem around the bottom of the blouse. Stitch close to the folded edge on the inside of the garment and press the hem from the inside.

20 Mark the first button position right at the top of the placket on the wearer's left, then one at the bust point (you can do this by putting the blouse on and indicating with a pin the fullest point of your bust, to avoid a gaping button placket). Distribute the buttons evenly in between, attaching the last button about 10 cm (4 in.) above the hem. Always go for an odd number of buttons! Make vertical buttonholes on the wearer's right front placket to correspond.

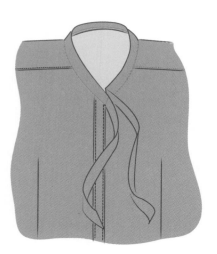

SPECIAL TECHNIQUE: WORKING WITH DELICATE FABRICS

If you have decided to use a delicate fabric such as silk, chiffon or georgette, we have some special tips for you.

○ When sewing, use a small needle size (60 or 70), lower your stitch length to between 2.2 and 2.5 to avoid puckering, and select a fine thread such as a polyester.

○ If your fabric is very slippery and won't lie still, try positioning it on top of some tissue paper and treat the tissue paper as part of the fabric: you can pin the pattern pieces to it, cut it out together and even sew with the tissue paper on the bottom. This gives the machine something to grip when the fabric is very slippery and afterwards you can gently rip the paper out of the seam.

○ To mark really fine fabric, you can sometimes get away with using a tracing wheel without carbon paper. Coloured markings on fine fabrics are often hard to get rid off, so if you need to mark things like darts on silk, this method works really well.

○ Regular pins will leave marks on very fine fabrics that won't disappear. You can avoid this by using extra-fine silk pins or by pinning within the seam allowances rather than within the pattern lines.

○ Spray starch can sometimes do wonders for fabrics that simply won't behave. Make sure you test it on a scrap before committing to this technique, as you do need to hand wash out the starch after your garment is finished. You only need to spray starch the area where you are working – for example, a row of pin tucks on a silk blouse.

○ For step-by-step instructions on how to finish your garment with a French seam, see page 26.

Sleep Set

With an elasticated waistband and shorts inspired by vintage tap pants, this pattern not only looks good but is also super comfortable to wear. Nothing in the bodice of this pattern is cut on the fold, so you can really make the most economical use of your fabric. This cosy and stylish set can also be made as an all-in-one romper version (see page 72) or as functional separates for mixing and matching. Why not try using different prints, or using up jersey remnants from your fabric stash?

TO MAKE THE SLEEP SET

Materials

- Sizes 4–10: 2 m (2¼ yd) fabric 115 cm (45 in.) wide or 2 m (2¼ yd) fabric 150 cm (60 in.) wide
- Sizes 12–18: 2.5 m (2¾ yd) fabric 115 cm (45 in.) wide or 2.3 m (2½ yd) fabric 150 cm (60 in.) wide
- Stay tape or ribbon
- 1 m (1 yd) elastic, 3 cm (1¼ in.) wide
- Ready-made bias binding or make your own with the pattern provided
- Basic sewing kit (see page 14)

Difficulty level

Confident beginner

Fabric suggestions

You can make this pattern in either a stretch or a woven fabric. We recommend lightweight jerseys with a good amount of stretch, such as (organic) cotton jersey, viscose jersey or wool jersey, interlock, stretch velvet, or a fine rib knit. You could also make it in a finer woven fabric such as lightweight cotton or silk for a more lingerie-like set; if so, sew with a French seam (see page 26).

Design notes

Use a 1.5-cm (⅝-in.) seam allowance throughout, unless otherwise stated.

Instructions are given for overlocking the seam allowances, but if you don't have an overlocker you can neaten the seam allowances by zigzagging them instead.

If you are making this pattern in a stretch fabric, you will need a bias binding in stretch as well.

We refer to French seams in this project, which require a different way of sewing a seam (see page 26). Decide beforehand whether you would like to do this technique so you can apply it when we suggest it.

Finished measurements	4	6	8	10	12	14	16	18
Front length (cm)	48	48.5	49	49.5	50	51	51.5	52
Front length (in.)	18⅞	19	19¼	19½	19⅝	20	20¼	20½
Bust (cm)	75.5	80.5	85.5	90.5	95.5	100.5	105.5	110.5
Bust (in.)	29¾	31⅝	33⅝	35⅝	37½	39½	41½	43½
Crotch length (cm)	72.5	75.5	78.5	81.5	84.5	87.5	90.5	93.5
Crotch length (in.)	28½	29¾	31	32	33¼	34½	35⅝	36¾
Inside leg (cm)	18.5	18.5	18.5	18.5	18.5	18.5	18.5	18.5
Inside leg (in.)	7¼	7¼	7¼	7¼	7¼	7¼	7¼	7¼
Outside leg (cm)	37	37.5	38	38.5	39	40	40.5	41
Outside leg (in.)	14½	14¾	15	15⅛	15⅜	15¾	16	16⅛

CUTTING GUIDE

SIZES 4–10 115 cm (45 in.) wide fabric

* Double one of your cuff pieces in size so it's not on the fold as this will waste less fabric

SIZES 12–18 115 cm (45 in.) wide fabric

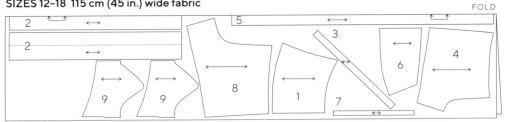

SIZES 4–10 150 cm (60 in.) wide fabric

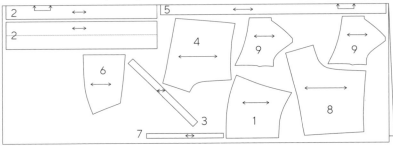

1   Back cami – cut 2
2   Leg cuff – cut 2 on the fold*
3   Binding – cut 1
4   Front leg – cut 2
5   Waistband – cut 1 on the fold
6   Front cami – cut 2
7   Rouleau strap – cut 2
8   Back leg – cut 2
9   Front bust – cut 4

SIZES 12–18 150 cm (60 in.) wide fabric

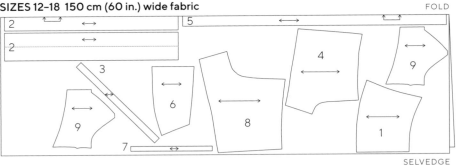

THE SEWING STARTS HERE

CAMI TOP

1 Staystitch the top and bottom of the front bust panels and the front bust lining pieces 1 cm (⅜ in.) from the raw edge. If you are sewing in a stretch fabric such as jersey, use stay tape rather than staystitching. This means you zigzag over a piece of non-stretchy tape within your seam allowance so that the edge won't stretch once you start assembling your garment.

2 Pin the bust darts on the front bust panels and front bust lining pieces and sew from the side edge to the point. Don't backstitch at the point of the dart: run off exactly where the dart finishes, leave a tail with your thread and tie it off by hand. This way you get a perfect point. Press the darts downwards.

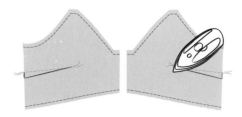

3 With right sides together, pin the front bust pieces together along the centre front. Sew, then press the seam open. Repeat with the front bust lining pieces.

....

TOP TIPS FOR SEWING STRETCH FABRICS

- Use a ballpoint needle.
- Use polyester thread to avoid the thread breaking when pulled.
- Use a narrow zigzag stitch or a twin needle stitch to give you a seam that allows for a bit of stretch; a straight stitch can't stretch at all.
- Try using a walking foot.

....

4 With right sides together, pin the cami fronts together along the centre front. Sew, then press the seam open. Overlock the seam allowances together and press the seam to either left or right. Repeat with the back cami pieces. If you're using a woven fabric, you could sew a French seam.

5 Matching the notches and matching the centre front seams to each other, pin the top of the front cami to the bottom of the main fabric front bust. Sew together, pivoting at the centre front seam. Press the seam open, then press the seam up towards the bust.

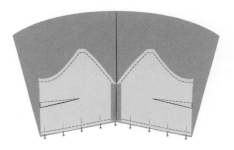

6 **Attach the straps**
Make the rouleau straps (see page 80). Pin one end of each strap to the front of the cami, pointing downwards. Tack in place 1 cm (⅜ in.) from the raw edge.

7 **Attach the lining**
With right sides together, matching the centre front seams, place the front bust lining on top of the cami bust. Pin along the top neckline, making sure you don't catch the straps elsewhere in the seam. Stitch together, pivoting at the centre front seam. Clip into the V at the centre front, taking care not to cut into the line of stitching; this allows the V to sit flat.

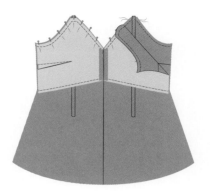

8 Trim the seam allowance down to 5 mm (¼ in.), press the seam allowances downwards and understitch the seam allowance to the bust lining. Using a bamboo pointer, push the area around the strap out to create a neat finish. If you are using a jersey or thicker fabric, clip into any corners to reduce bulk.

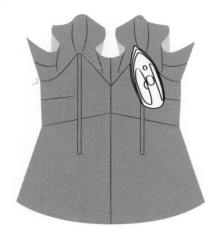

9 Press the unattached edge of the bust lining towards the wrong side by 1.5 cm (⅝ in.).

10 Turn the bust lining to the inside of the cami. Roll and press the understitched V-neck seam slightly towards the inside. Pin the sides of the bust lining to the sides of the cami bust. Tack or stitch in place using a 1-cm (⅜-in.) seam allowance, so that you can treat the cami and the lining as one piece. Slipstitch the pressed-under bottom edge of the bust lining to the cami by hand or stitch in the ditch (see page 81, step 12).

11 Pin the loose ends of the straps to the notches on the back of the bodice, with raw edges and right sides together (the straps should be upside down, as for the cami front in step 7). Try on the cami to see if you are happy with the strap length, then stitch in place with a 1-cm (⅜-in.) seam allowance.

12 Make your bias binding with the pattern piece provided; alternatively you can use ready-made bias binding. Pin and sew the binding along the raw edges of the outside top edge of the back cami, finishing at the side seams, sandwiching the straps in between. Finish it so the binding is entirely on the inside of your cami top; see Special Technique, page 71, Bias Binding Sewn on with Two Seams.

13 Attach front and back
With right sides together, lay the cami front on top of the cami back. The notches on the cami back match the dart and underbust seam. Pin the sides together, stitch and press the seams open. Overlock the seam allowances together at a foot's width. If you're using a woven fabric, you could sew a French seam.

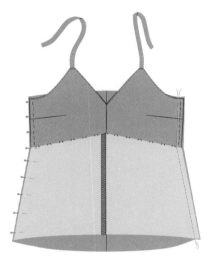

14 Hem the bottom of your cami top by pressing 5 mm (¼ in.), then 1 cm (⅜ in.) to the wrong side and stitching in place.

SHORTS

15 Place one pair of front and back leg pieces right sides together. Pin and sew the side seam and inside leg seam. Overlock the seam allowances together at a foot's width and press towards the back. Repeat with the remaining pair of leg pieces.

16 Turn one leg right side out and leave the other one wrong side out. Matching the inner leg seams and the notches along the curve, slide one leg inside the other, right sides together. Pin and sew the crotch seam all along the curve. Overlock the seam allowances together at a foot's width. Turn the shorts right side out.

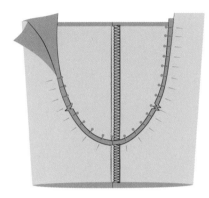

17 Attach the leg cuffs
Fold the leg cuff in half, with right sides together, and sew together at the short ends. Press the seam open without finishing off the seam allowances. Repeat on the other cuff. Fold the cuffs in half lengthways, with wrong sides together, and press. Machine tack the open edge within the seam allowance.

18 With right sides together, matching the side seam of the cuffs with the inside leg seams, pin the tacked edge of the cuffs to the raw edge of the shorts legs. Sew all around. Overlock the seam allowances together. Fold the cuffs down and press the seams up towards the legs.

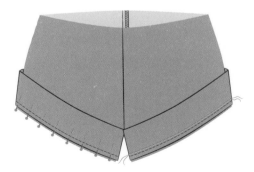

19 **Assemble the waistband**
With right sides together, pin the narrow sides of the waistband together and stitch. Press the seam open without finishing the seam allowances. Fold the waistband in half lengthways, with wrong sides together, and press. Machine tack the remaining open edge of the waistband within the seam allowance, leaving a 3-cm gap (1¼-in.) in the seam.

20 Matching the waistband seam with one of the shorts side seams, pin the tacked edge of the waistband to the shorts, right sides together, all the way around the raw edge of the shorts waist. Sew in place, leaving the same 3-cm (1¼-in.) gap to be able to insert your elastic.

21 Attach a safety pin to the waistband elastic and feed it through the channel on the shorts. When you have reached the other end, overlap the two ends of the elastic by 1 cm (³⁄₈ in.), zigzag them together and sew the gap in your waistband shut. Overlock the seam allowances together at a foot's width and press down towards the shorts.

SPECIAL TECHNIQUE: ATTACHING BIAS BINDING

Bias binding is a great way to finish off exposed seam allowances, to invisibly finish armholes and necklines without having to use a facing, or to decoratively finish curved edges. We recommend that you staystitch any curves before you apply bias binding.

Sewn on with one seam

With this method, you can stitch your bias binding on with only one stitch line! As the binding is visible on both sides of the bound edge, this technique is suitable for decorative binding and for finishing seam allowances that are visible.

1 If you are making binding yourself, fold the long raw edges of your bias strip in to the centre (this is how it arrives if it's ready-made). Then fold the bias binding in half lengthwise, wrong sides together, with a step: one side should be about 3 mm (⅛ in.) wider than the other. Press well.

2 Slot the binding around the raw edge that you are binding. The wider half should lie underneath. Topstitch from the right side; you will automatically catch the other side of the bias as it's a little bit wider.

Sewn on with two seams

With this method, the binding is visible only on the inside of the bound edge. It is really suitable for necklines and armholes.

1 Open out the bias binding, pin it to the outside of your garment with right sides together, and sew in the first crease line.

2 Fold the bias binding completely to the inside of the garment and press really well. Then slipstitch the other edge of the binding in place by hand. Alternatively, topstitch it in place from the right side; this stitching would be visible on the outside of your garment.

Romper

With its elasticised waistband, this vintage-inspired romper is the perfect Sunday loungewear. We recommend using a cosy, stretchy fabric such as jersey for comfort and style.

Materials

- 2.8 m (3⅛ yd) fabric 115 cm (45 in.) wide
- 1 m (1 yd) elastic, 3 cm (1¼ in.) wide
- Ready-made bias binding or make your own with the pattern provided
- Basic sewing kit (see page 14)

Difficulty level

Confident beginner

1 Cut out the pieces, using the shorter cutting line for the cami front and back pattern pieces.

2 Make up the cami and shorts, following steps 1–18 of the Sleep Set on pages 66–69.

3 Pin and sew one waistband back and one waistband front piece together along the side seams. Press the seams open without finishing off the seam allowances. Repeat with the remaining two pieces so that you have two identical, single-layer waistbands. Aligning the side seams in the waistband with the side seams of the cami, sandwich the two waistbands right sides together, with the raw hem of the cami in between. Stitch in place.

4 Turn the waistband down, press, and machine tack around the remaining open edge, leaving a 3-cm (1¼-in.) gap at one of the side seams. Now attach the waistband to the shorts as described in step 20 of the Sleep Set and insert the elastic as in step 21. Overlock the seam allowances together at a foot's width and press down towards the shorts.

1	Waistband front – cut 2	**6**	Waistband – cut 1 on the fold
2	Waistband back – cut 2	**7**	Front cami – cut 2
3	Back leg – cut 2	**8**	Rouleau strap – cut 2
4	Leg cuff – cut 2 on the fold	**9**	Back cami – cut 2
5	Binding – cut 1	**10**	Front leg – cut 2
		11	Front bust – cut 4

115 cm (45 in.) wide fabric

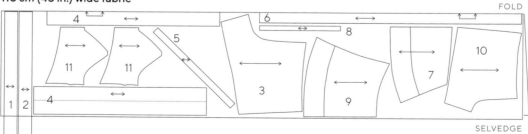

*Cutting note: unfold your fabric to fit the waistbands.

Midi Wrap Skirt

This beautiful wrap skirt is a contemporary shape and great for all occasions. You can wear it with a plain T-shirt and sneakers for a pared-down look, or to work with a crisp shirt or a turtleneck. The angle on the front panel makes for a slight bias cut, so this will really test your accuracy when stitching: if you stretch it, it will end up looking slightly fluted.

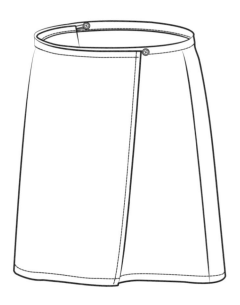

TO MAKE THE MIDI WRAP SKIRT

Materials

- Sizes 4–10: 1.8 m (2 yd) fabric 150 cm (60 in.) wide
- Sizes 12–18: 2.2 m (2⅜ yd) fabric 150 cm (60 in.) wide
- 20 cm (8 in.) interfacing
- 2 flat buttons
- Basic sewing kit (see page 14)
- Rouleau turner (handy but not essential)

Difficulty level

Confident beginners and improvers

Fabric suggestions

Medium-weight cotton, drill, denim, cotton satin, corduroy, brocade

Design notes

Use a 1.5-cm (⅝-in.) seam allowance throughout, unless otherwise stated.

Instructions are given for overlocking the seam allowances, but if you don't have an overlocker you can neaten the seam allowances by zigzagging them instead.

Finished measurements	4	6	8	10	12	14	16	18
Centre front length (cm)	74.5	74.5	74.5	74.5	74.5	74.5	74.5	74.5
Centre front length (in.)	29½	29½	29½	29½	29½	29½	29½	29½
Back length (cm)	76.5	76.5	76.5	76.5	76.5	76.5	76.5	76.5
Back length (in.)	30	30	30	30	30	30	30	30
Waist (cm)	69.5	74.5	79.5	84.5	89.5	94.5	99.5	104.5
Waist (in.)	27⅜	29⅜	31¼	33¼	35¼	37¼	39⅛	41⅛
Low hip (cm)	92.5	97.5	102.5	107.5	112.5	117.5	122.5	127.5
Low hip (in.)	36½	38⅜	40⅜	42⅜	44¼	46¼	48¼	50¼

CUTTING GUIDE

SIZES 4–10

150 cm (60 in.) wide fabric

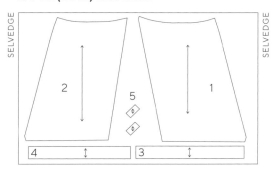

150 cm (60 in.) wide fabric

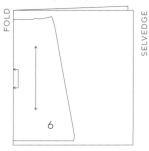

Interfacing

SIZES 12–28

150 cm (60 in.) wide fabric

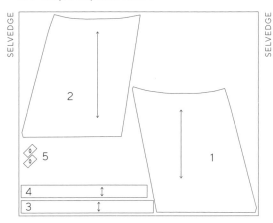

150 cm (60 in.) wide fabric

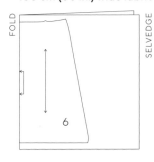

Interfacing

1 Left front – cut 1

2 Right front – cut 1

3 Right waistband – cut 1 in
main and 1 in interfacing

4 Left waistband – cut 1 in
main and 1 in interfacing

5 Rouleau loop – cut 2

6 Back – cut 1 on the fold

THE SEWING STARTS HERE

1 **Prepare the pieces**
Following the manufacturer's instructions, apply interfacing to the wrong side of the left and right waistbands.

2 **Construct the skirt**
Mark and pin the two darts on the back skirt. Sew from the waist to the point. Don't backstitch at the point of the dart: run off exactly where the dart finishes, leave a tail with your thread and tie it off. Press the darts towards the centre back.

3 With right sides together, pin the left front skirt to the back skirt panel, taking care not to stretch the angled edge. Overlock the seam allowances together at a foot's width and press towards the back of the skirt. Repeat with the right front skirt, so that you end up with all three skirt pieces sewn together.

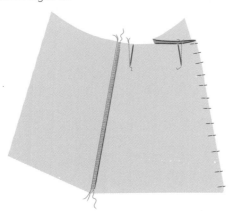

4 Turn up and press a double 1.5-cm (⅝-in.) hem along the bottom of the skirt. Pin in place and sew close to the folded edge from the wrong side.

5 Finish both front edges of the skirt by turning under and pressing a double 1.5-cm (⅝-in.) hem. Be very careful not to stretch these edges when you press them, as they're on the bias. Use plenty of pins to prevent a fluted edge and stitch close to the folded edge on the wrong side of the skirt. Press the hemmed edges from the wrong side.

6 **Construct the waistband**
With right sides together, pin the left and right waistbands together along the centre back seam. Sew, then press the seam allowances open without finishing the raw edges.

7 Press the waistband in half lengthwise, wrong sides together. Then press one of the outer edges of the waistband to the wrong side by 1.5 cm (⅝ in.), using the following method: with right sides together, position the waistband on the skirt, making sure you have the left and right halves of the waistband against the corresponding sides of the skirt. The long edge of the waistband that isn't lying against the skirt waist is the one you are to press.

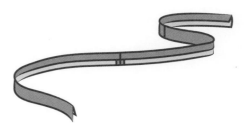

8 Attach the waistband
With right sides together, pin the unpressed edge of the waistband to the waist of the skirt. Make sure you match the waistband notches to the notches at the centre back and centre front of the skirt, and then match the dart and side seam notches. Sew the waistband in place, then press the seam allowances up towards the waistband.

9 Construct the rouleau loops
Fold the rouleau loops in half lengthways, right sides together, and sew down the long unfolded edge. Trim the seam allowance to 2–3 mm (a scant ⅛ in.). Use a rouleau turner to pull the loops through to the right side and press, with the seam line on the edge.

TOP TIP

If you don't have a rouleau turner, you can leave a long tail of thread at the end of your machine stitch, thread it through a large, blunt needle (such as a darning needle), feed the needle through the tube and out the other end. Gently pull it and the loop should start turning in on itself. You can also encase a piece of cord in the loop when you machine stitch down the long edge. Sew with a zipper foot and anchor the cord by sewing horizontally across the top short edge as well. Then use the cord to gently pull your loop right side out.

10 On the outside edges of the right side of the waistband, place the rouleau loops so that the loops face in towards the centre back of the skirt. Pin the loops in place and tack them within the seam allowance so that they don't move.

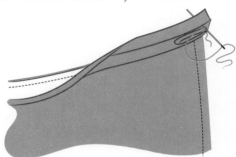

11 Finish the waistband
Fold the right sides of your waistband together (you should no longer be able to see the rouleau loops) and stitch the short edges. Trim the seam allowance down to 5 mm (¼ in.), turn the waistband right side out again and your rouleau loops will appear on the outside.

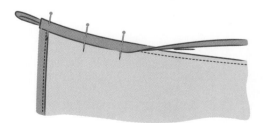

12 Pin the pressed-under edge of the waistband to the skirt by pinning through the waist seam on the outside and catching the waistband edge on the inside. Pin all the way around, then stitch in the ditch from the outside of the skirt: line up the needle with the crease of the seam and stitch all the way around, catching the waistband on the back. When you are finished, you should not be able to see this stitching on the outside of the skirt.

13 Referring to the pattern, mark the button positions on the waistband. Sew one button on the inside of the right waistband and one on the outside of the left waistband.

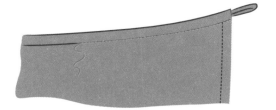

VARIATION

Mini Scrap Skirt

This mini version of the wrap skirt is the ultimate scrap buster, as it uses left-over fabrics from previous projects to create a colourful patchwork: all you have to do is make your patchwork big enough to fit the shorter front and back pattern pieces. Don't cut the waistband from the patchwork, however – you might well end up with bulky seams inside it that will look unsightly and feel uncomfortable.

Materials

- Lots of fabric scraps for the patchwork
- 0.5 – 1 m (20 in. – 1 yd) plain fabric for waistband, depending on size
- 0.5 – 1 m (20 in. – 1 yd) interfacing, depending on size
- 2 flat buttons
- Basic sewing kit (see page 14)
- Rouleau turner (handy but not essential)

For details of how many of each piece to cut, refer to the cutting guide on page 77.

Difficulty level

Confident beginners and improvers

1 Cut your chosen fabrics into squares or rectangles, or use your imagination to create interesting shapes. Make your shapes at least 15 cm (6 in.) long and wide. Arrange them to make an attractive patchwork.

2 Place two fabric pieces right sides together and stitch along one edge, taking a 1.5-cm (⅝-in.) seam allowance. Press the seam open, and overlock or zigzag the seam allowances.

3 Repeat until the pieces have been stitched together and you have a piece of fabric that will comfortably fit your skirt pattern pieces.

4 Cut out the pattern pieces from the patchwork, using the shorter cutting line on the front and back pattern pieces. Cut out the waistband pieces from a plain piece of fabric.

5 Make up the skirt, following the instructions for the Midi Wrap Skirt on pages 78–81.

Finished measurements	4	6	8	10	12	14	16	18
Centre front length (cm)	40	40	40	40	40	40	40	40
Centre front length (in.)	15¾	15¾	15¾	15¾	15¾	15¾	15¾	15¾
Back length (cm)	42	42	42	42	42	42	42	42
Back length (in.)	16½	16½	16½	16½	16½	16½	16½	16½
Waist (cm)	69.5	74.5	79.5	84.5	89.5	94.5	99.5	104.5
Waist (in.)	27⅜	29⅜	31¼	33¼	35¼	37¼	39¼	41¼
Low hip (cm)	92.5	97.5	102.5	107.5	112.5	117.5	122.5	127.5
Low hip (in.)	36½	38⅜	40⅜	42⅜	44¼	46¼	48¼	50¼

WHAT TO DO WITH OFFCUTS

Fabric waste is a big problem in the fashion industry and luckily it's one of the areas over which you have more control when you make your own clothes at home. Any leftover fabric can be called an offcut, and what you do with those offcuts is up to you. For tips on what to do with bigger pieces of fabrics, see Recycle and Re-use Clothing on page 186.

AVOID OFFCUTS

Our first tip is to avoid offcuts as much as possible. The way to do this is to cut projects out economically and not buy too much fabric. When you cut out your pattern pieces, lay them out as close together as possible, without distorting the grain or the print. This enables you to use the least amount of fabric, leaving you with even fewer offcuts or bigger offcuts, which are more useful.

We usually cut on the fold in dressmaking, which means we lay out a pattern on a folded piece of fabric so we get two of each by cutting once: two sleeves, two trouser legs, etc. This is definitely the easiest and quickest way to do it, but it not always the most economical way. By cutting on a single layer you can usually save some fabric – sometimes even up to half a metre (yard). This will also save you money.

RE-USE OFFCUTS

Some offcuts are big enough to reuse into something else. You can use them for smaller homeware projects, tote bags, hair scrunchies, headbands, clutch bags, toiletry bags, baby clothes or pencil cases. You can also think about making fabric versions of things you have in your home that you normally use single-use items for, such as cleaning cloths, flannels, baby wipes, and make-up removers. These are all great sustainable scrap busters!

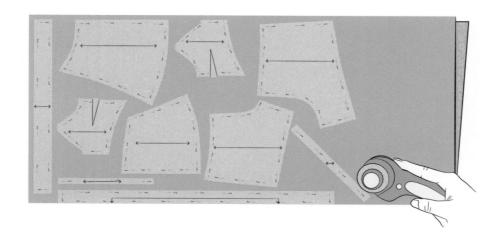

Have a look at the pressing ham on page 100 for a great project that uses up lots of small offcuts that can't be used for anything else.

RECYCLE OFFCUTS

Some places will take offcuts for specific purposes: textile offcuts can be turned into housing insulation or they can be used by quilting groups. Maybe you know of a sustainable fashion brand that can use them in their designs?

PATCHWORK

You can turn sizeable offcuts into a new material by patchworking them together. This is a great idea for smaller garments, such as the mini wrap skirt on page 82 or the jacket on page 126, but you can also think of items like a pouffe for your home or a tote bag.

INFORM AND SHARE

Did you make a great project using offcuts? Or do you run a business that deals with textile offcuts? Inform and inspire each other so we can learn from one another. Using offcuts sometimes requires some imagination and it's a great thing to be able to share this with other people so we can all become more creative with our textile waste. It's not waste until you dispose of it – so the longer your textiles can live, the better.

Denim Apron

Denim is a great fabric, but it's very labour- and water-intensive to produce, so the longer we can make use of it the better. Here, we're turning a pair of unloved old jeans into an apron, suitable for men and women. We've shown a very simple transformation, but the possibilities are endless: you could add hardware such as rivets for a really industrial look, re-use the pockets, play with the shape of the apron, topstitch in a contrasting colour, or even combine elements from different jeans.

Materials

- Pair of full-length jeans
- Basic sewing kit (see page 14)
- Unpicker or sharp small snips
- Denim needle (size 90)

Note: You may want to use a different material for the waist tie.

1 Using both the legs of your jeans to create your apron front: unpick the inside leg seam of both legs all the way up to the crotch and cut them away from your jeans. Pin the longest sides together and sew down the middle. Press your seams open so it lies flat. Mark out the shape of your apron top at the narrowest part of the leg. Cut out, unfold the leg and there is your apron front!

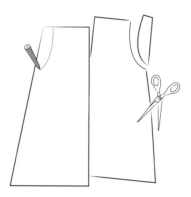

TOP TIP

You need a generous amount of fabric for this project, so skinny jeans might not be the best choice.

2 Finish any raw edges. Denim is very thick, which makes it difficult to stitch a double-turned hem, so overlock the edges and press and stitch a single hem.

3 Make straps to go around the waist and the neck. We used the denim waistband as the neck strap and made waist ties from cotton tape. Re-use interesting parts of your jeans to create features on the apron – for example, placing the jeans' back pockets on the apron front.

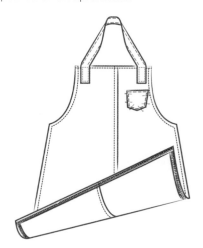

Summer Dress

Easy to dress up or down on sunny days, but also great with tights and boots in colder weather, this dress has everything you need to become your go-to wardrobe staple. With a playful smocking panel around the waist, it looks and feels great to wear and is based on popular 1940s dress shapes.

TO MAKE THE SUMMER DRESS

Materials

- Sizes 4–10: 2.2 m (2½ yd) fabric 150 cm (60 in.) wide
- Sizes 12–18: 2.7 m (3 yd) fabric 150 cm (60 in.) wide
- 25 cm (10 in.) interfacing
- 51-cm (20-in.) invisible zip
- Elastic bobbin thread for the smocking
- 3–5 decorative front buttons (optional)

Difficulty level

Confident beginners and improvers

Fabric suggestions

We suggest using a fabric with plenty of drape, such as viscose/rayon, bamboo silk, tencel, crepe, silk, crepe de Chine or georgette.

Design notes

Use a 1.5-cm (⅝-in.) seam allowance throughout, unless otherwise stated.

Instructions are given for overlocking the seam allowances, but if you don't have an overlocker you can neaten the seam allowances by zigzagging them instead.

Finished measurements	**4**	**6**	**8**	**10**	**12**	**14**	**16**	**18**
Front length (cm)	99	99.5	100	100.5	101	102	102.5	103
Front length (in.)	39	39⅛	39⅜	39½	39¾	40⅛	40⅜	40½
Back length (cm)	98.5	99	99.5	100	100.5	101.5	102	102.5
Back length (in.)	38¾	39	39⅛	39⅜	39½	40	40⅛	40⅜
Bust (cm)	91	96	101	106	111	116	121	126
Bust (in.)	35⅞	37¾	39¾	41¾	43¾	45⅝	47⅝	49⅝
Waist (cm)	75.5	80.5	85.5	90.5	95.5	100.5	105.5	110.5
Waist (in.)	29¾	31¾	33⅝	35⅝	37½	39½	41½	43½
Sleeve length long (cm)	60	60.5	61	61.5	62	62.5	63	63.5
Sleeve length long (in.)	23⅝	23⅞	24	24¼	24½	24⅝	24⅞	25
Sleeve length short (cm)	17	17.5	18	18.5	19	19.5	20	20.5
Sleeve length short (in.)	6¾	6⅞	7	7¼	7½	7⅝	7⅞	8

CUTTING GUIDE

SIZES 4–10 150 cm (60 in.) wide fabric

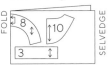

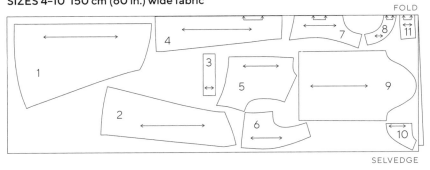

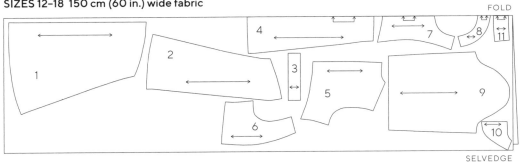

SIZES 12–18 150 cm (60 in.) wide fabric

Interfacing

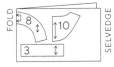

1   Back skirt – cut 2

2   Side front skirt – cut 2

3   Cuff (long-sleeved version only) – cut 2 in main and 2 in interfacing

4   Centre front skirt – cut 1 on the fold

5   Back bodice – cut 2

6   Side bodice – cut 2

7   Centre front bodice – cut 1 on the fold

8   Front facing – cut 1 on the fold in main and 1 in interfacing

9   Sleeve – cut 2

10   Back facing – cut 2 in main and 2 in interfacing

11   Smocking panel – cut 1 on the fold

THE SEWING STARTS HERE

1 Prepare the pieces
Following the manufacturer's instructions, apply interfacing to the wrong side of the back and front facings. Staystitch the neckline on the back bodices and the centre front bodice 1 cm (⅜ in.) from the raw edge. Also staystitch the centre front bodice and the side bodices along the curved vertical edges, 1 cm (⅜ in.) from the raw edge. Clip into the side bodice seam allowances without going over the stay stitches.

2 Assemble the bodice
With right sides together, pin the darts on the back bodice pieces and stitch from the waist to the point. Don't backstitch at the point of the dart: run off exactly where the dart finishes, leave a tail with your thread and tie it off by hand. This way you get a perfect point. Press the darts towards the side.

3 With right sides together, matching the notches, pin the side bodices to the centre front bodice. Sew, then overlock the seam allowances together at a foot's width and press the seams towards the sides, using a tailor's ham.

....

TOP TIP

For more information on sewing curved seams, see page 25.

....

4 With right sides together, pin the back bodice pieces to the front bodice at the shoulder seams and side seams. Sew all four seams. Overlock the side seams together at a foot's width and press towards the back. Press the shoulder seams open and overlock the seam allowances separately.

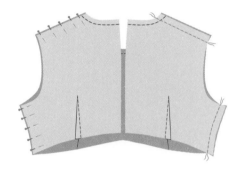

5 Assemble the sleeves
For both the long- and the short-sleeved options, fold the sleeves in half, right sides together, and pin the underarm seams. Sew, overlock the seam allowances separately and press the seams open. For the short-sleeved version, which doesn't have sleeve cuffs, turn up and press a double 1.5-cm (⅝-in.) hem. Pin in place and sew.

6 If you are making the long-sleeved option with cuffs, turn to page 149, steps 6–9.

7 With right sides together, insert the sleeves into the bodice. Pin in place, matching the notches and matching the side seam of the bodice with the sleeve underarm seam. Sew, then overlock the seam allowances together at a foot's width. Press the seams towards the bodice.

8 **Gather the bodice**
Run two lines of gathering stitches across the bottom of the centre front bodice, between the bust seams, Use the biggest stitch on your machine (don't backstitch) and stitch one line on top of the pattern line and one line a foot's width into the seam allowance. Draw up the gathered section to measure 10 cm (4 in.). Run two lines of gathering stitches across the top of the centre front skirt, between the side front skirt seams, and draw it up to 10 cm (4 in.) as well.

9 On the smocking panel, work four lines of smocking 1 cm (⅜ in.) apart (see Special Technique on page 97), as marked on the pattern. The panel should end up being 10 cm (4 in.) in width.

10 With right sides together, pin the bottom edge of the smocked panel to the top edge of the centre front skirt. (The skirt panel was gathered to fit the smocked panel in step 8.) Sew and overlock the seam allowances together at a foot's width. Press the smocked panel up and the seam allowances down towards the hem. Your centre front skirt is now one unit.

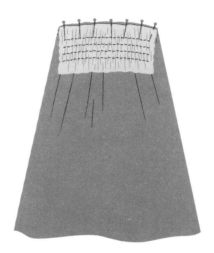

11 With right sides together, pin the centre front skirt panel to the side skirt panels. Sew the side seams, overlock the seams together at a foot's width and press towards the back. Pin the entire front skirt (consisting of three panels) to the back skirt at the side seams, with right sides together. Sew, overlock the seam allowances together at a foot's width and press the seams towards the back. Your skirt is now one piece, remaining open at the centre back.

12 Assemble the bodice and skirt
With right sides together, matching up the seams on the bodice with the seams on the skirt and matching the notches in the back bodice with the notches in the back skirt, pin and sew the bodice to the skirt. Overlock the seam allowances together at a foot's width. Press the seam down towards the hem.

13 Overlock both edges of the centre back from the neckline to the dress hem.

14 Assemble the facing
With right sides together, pin the front facing to the back facing at the shoulder seams. Sew and press the seams open. Overlock the outer edge of the facing.

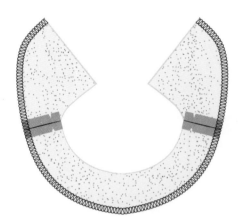

15 With right sides together, matching the facing shoulder seam to the bodice shoulder seam, pin the facing to your dress. Sew, clip into the neckline, then trim down the seam allowance to 5 mm (¼ in.) and clip into the curved seam allowance. Turn the facing to the inside of the dress or blouse and understitch the seam to the facing (see page 152, step 19).

16 Finish the dress
Insert an invisible zip in the centre back seam (see page 28). Hand sew the facing along the zip tape (see page 152, step 22). On the inside of the garment, hand stitch the facing to the bodice shoulder seam and do the same at the centre front to hold it in place inside the bodice.

17 Hang your dress up for a day to allow the hem to drop. Give the garment a final press, then sew a double 1.5-cm (⅝-in.) hem.

18 If you wish, stitch 3–5 small buttons down the front, spacing them evenly.

SPECIAL TECHNIQUE: SMOCKING/SHIRRING

Smocking is traditionally done by hand and is a decorative gathering technique used to control fullness in a garment. As a machine technique it's typically done with shirring elastic on the bobbin thread and called shirring rather than smocking. More elaborate, decorative patterns are usually defined as smocking, whereas straight, elastic lines are commonly called shirring.

It's important to make up the smocking before you assemble your garment, so that you can make sure the smocked area is the exact size you need. Mark your smocking lines really carefully before starting. You need a sewing machine, elastic sewing thread for the bobbin and regular thread for the needle.

1 Wind your bobbin with the elastic thread by hand: aim for a little bit of tension when you do this, without fully using the elasticity of the thread. Distribute the thread evenly around the bobbin, and set up the rest of your machine as per usual.

2 Lower the needle tension on your machine and do a sample stitch: you should see the elastic bobbin thread on the back and only the needle thread on the front.

3 Start your first line, and don't backstitch. After a few stitches, tie up the needle and bobbin threads by hand at the start of your line. When you reach the end of your first line, tie the thread ends by hand again instead of backstitching.

4 Sew all consecutive rows by pulling the fabric flat, to achieve even lines.

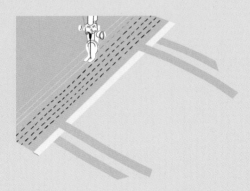

TOP TIPS

○ If your stitches are not gathering and the elastic looks loose on the back: change your bobbin tension.

○ If the needle thread looks as if it's only looping around the elastic on the back: change your needle tension.

○ If you are sewing lots of rows, check your bobbin thread regularly, as the elastic thread will run out much quicker than you think! You won't be able to restart a smocking stitch halfway through once the bobbin thread has run out.

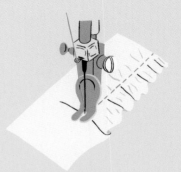

VARIATION

Blouse

This blouse is the perfect wardrobe staple: wear it with your favourite jeans for a casual look or pair it with slim-fitting cigarette trousers for a chic office outfit. Why not try colour blocking the panels? For the cooler autumn and winter months, make it with long sleeves that gather into the cuffs.

Materials

- Sizes 4–10: 1.4 m (1½ yd) fabric 150 cm (60 in.) wide
- Sizes 12–18: 1.7 m (1⅞ yd) fabric 150 cm (60 in.) wide
- 25 cm (10 in.) interfacing
- 55-cm (22- in.) invisible zip
- Elastic bobbin thread for the smocking
- Basic sewing kit (see page 14)

For details of how many of each piece to cut, refer to the cutting guide on page 91.

Difficulty level

Confident beginners and improvers

1 Cut out the pieces, using the shorter cutting line on the back, centre front and side front skirt panels. If you are making the short-sleeved version, do not cut the sleeve cuffs.

2 Make up the blouse, following steps 1–18 of the Summer Dress on pages 92–96.

SIZES 4–10 150 cm (60 in.) wide fabric

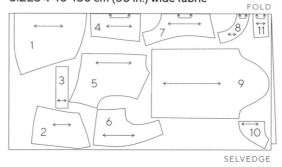

Interfacing

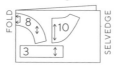

SIZES 12–18 150 cm (60 in.) wide fabric

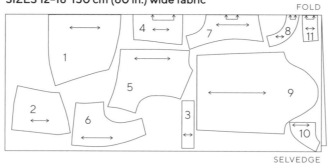

Interfacing

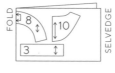

Pressing Ham

A pressing ham is a tool to help you iron curves. It's an essential part of your toolkit if you want to get serious about dressmaking. They can be expensive to buy, though, so follow the steps below to make your own from leftover scraps. You could make different shapes of hams to suit different ironing needs, such as a round one for curves and an elongated one for sleeves.

TOP TIP

A pressing ham needs to be really sturdy and well stuffed, so it takes a lot of scraps to make one – so this transformation project is the perfect scrap buster. Keep a bin or a basket in your sewing space and collect all small fabric offcuts for projects such as this.

Materials

- 2 pieces of fabric, roughly 50 x 50 cm (20 x 20 in.)
- Lots of finely cut fabric scraps for the filling
- Paper for pattern
- Pencil
- Basic sewing kit (see page 14)

1 Wash your pieces of fabric to prevent any shrinkage: the pressing ham will endure a lot of steam during its use, so you don't want it to shrink!

2 Draw an elongated egg-shaped pattern piece, about 35 cm (14 in.) long and 25 cm (10 in.) wide. Cut it out twice in your fabric. If you are making a sleeve ham, draw a pattern that is roughly 35 cm (14 in.) long and about 20 cm (8 in.) wide.

3 Pin the elongated egg-shaped fabric pieces right sides together and sew with a small seam allowance, leaving a 10-cm (4-in.) gap so that you can stuff the ham. Clip into any curves.

4 Turn the ham right side out, stuff it really tightly with shredded fabric scraps, then neatly slipstitch the gap closed.

Carnaby Coat

This is the ultimate work-to-weekend coat, a timeless staple that will never go out of style. Featuring faux buttons down the centre, a flat collar and deep retro-style patch pockets, it can be made to suit all seasons, depending on your fabric choice. If you haven't sewn a coat before this is the perfect pattern to start with, as it has a straightforward shape and no internal pockets or complicated collar.

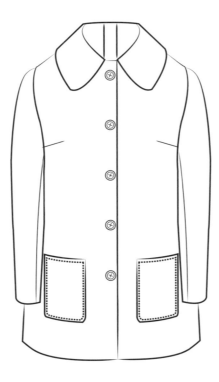

TO MAKE THE CARNABY COAT

Materials

- Sizes 4–10: 2.2m (2½ yd) fabric 150 cm (60 in.) wide
- Sizes 12–18: 2.7 m (3 yd) fabric 150 cm (60 in.) wide
- Sizes 4–10: 1.6 m (1¾ yd) lining fabric 150 cm (60 in.) wide
- Sizes 12–18: 1.9 m (2 yd) lining fabric 150 cm (60 in.) wide
- 1 m (1 yd) interfacing
- 3–5 coat buttons
- 3–5 big poppers

Difficulty level

Confident beginners and improvers

Fabric suggestions

The fabric really makes this design: you can either play safe or go all out with your choice of print, colour and material. For a warmer coat, choose from tweed, wool, melton wool or corduroy. For a spring coat, go for twill, upcycled denim, gabardine, heavyweight linen or heavyweight cotton.

Design notes

Use a 1.5-cm (⅝-in.) seam allowance throughout, unless otherwise stated.

This is a lined coat, so you don't need to finish the seams by overlocking or zigzagging, as this will only create bulk. If you have a main fabric that you think might fray too much, then overlock or zigzag after having pressed the seam allowances as per the instructions.

Finished measurements	4	6	8	10	12	14	16	18
Front length (cm)	84	84.5	85	86	86.5	87	87.5	88
Front length (in.)	33	33¼	33½	33⅞	34	34¼	34½	34⅝
Back length (cm)	79	79.5	80	80.5	81	82	82.5	83
Back length (in.)	31	31¼	31½	31⅝	31⅞	32¼	32½	32⅝
Bust (cm)	96	101	106	111	116	121	126	131
Bust (in.)	37¾	39¾	41¾	43¾	45¾	47¾	49¾	51¾
Waist (cm)	96	101	106	111	116	121	126	131
Waist (in.)	37¾	39¾	41¾	43¾	45¾	47¾	49¾	51¾
Sleeve length (cm)	63	63.5	64	64.5	65	65.5	66	66.5
Sleeve length (in.)	24¾	25	25¼	25⅜	25½	25¾	26	26¼

CUTTING GUIDE

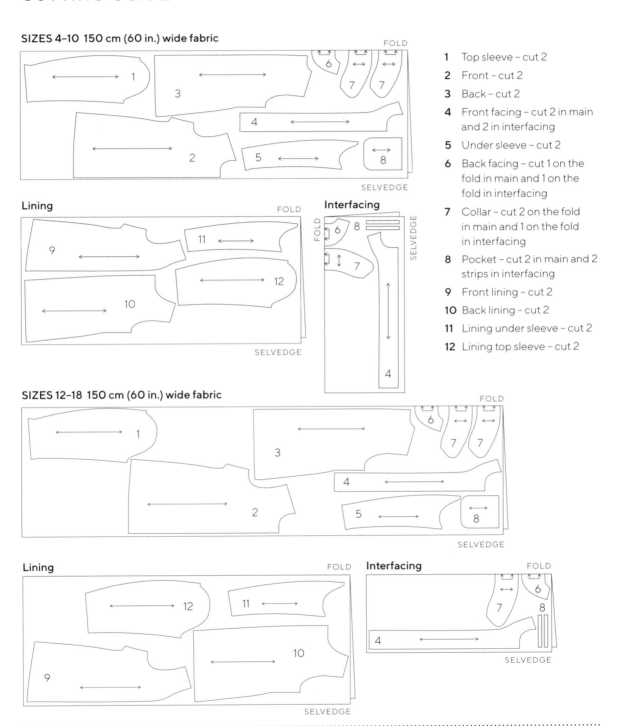

SIZES 4–10 150 cm (60 in.) wide fabric

Lining

Interfacing

1. Top sleeve – cut 2
2. Front – cut 2
3. Back – cut 2
4. Front facing – cut 2 in main and 2 in interfacing
5. Under sleeve – cut 2
6. Back facing – cut 1 on the fold in main and 1 on the fold in interfacing
7. Collar – cut 2 on the fold in main and 1 on the fold in interfacing
8. Pocket – cut 2 in main and 2 strips in interfacing
9. Front lining – cut 2
10. Back lining – cut 2
11. Lining under sleeve – cut 2
12. Lining top sleeve – cut 2

SIZES 12–18 150 cm (60 in.) wide fabric

Lining

Interfacing

THE SEWING STARTS HERE

1 Prepare the pieces
Staystitch the neckline of the front and back coat pieces 1 cm (⅜ in.) from the raw edge. Following the manufacturer's instructions, apply interfacing to the wrong side of the front and back facings. If you are adding a collar and pockets, interface one of the collar pieces and apply a 2-cm (¾-in.) strip of interfacing to the wrong side of each pocket along the top edge, 1 cm (⅜ in.) away from the raw edge. Mark the bust darts on the front and front lining pieces.

2 Assemble the front and back
Pin the bust darts on the front and front lining pieces and sew from the side seam to the point. Don't backstitch at the point of the dart: run off exactly where the dart finishes, leave a tail with your thread and tie it off by hand. This way you get a perfect point. Press the darts down towards the bottom of the coat.

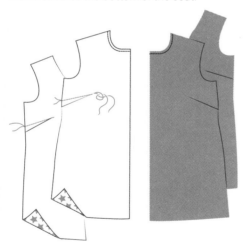

3 With right sides together, match up the centre back notches on the back pieces. Pin and sew, then press the seam open. Repeat for the back lining pieces. On the centre back of the lining, keeping the right sides together, sew 4 cm (1½ in.) down the pleat line indicated on your pattern. Press the top of the pleat in place from the right side of the fabric. This material will allow for extra movement in the coat.

4 With right sides together, pin the fronts to the back, matching the notches on the fronts to the notches on the back at the side and shoulder seams. Sew, then press the seams open. Repeat with the front and back lining pieces.

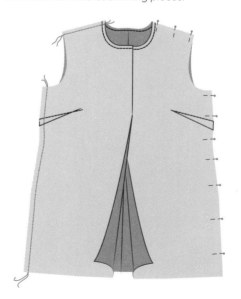

5 **Add the pockets**
Along the top edge of the pockets, press 1 cm (⅜ in.) to the wrong side, then press under the 2 cm (¾ in.) interfacing to create a strong top edge; see page 178, steps 3–4. Topstitch in place. Press 1.5 cm (⅝ in.) to the wrong side around the side and bottom edges of the pockets. Pin the pockets to the front of the coat and topstitch in place around the sides and bottom edges, 5 mm (¼ in.) from the pocket edges. You can also machine tack the entire outside edge of the pocket within the seam allowance as a pressing guide, or slightly pull the thread to encourage the curves to fold in.

6 **Assemble the sleeves**
With right sides together, matching the notches, pin and sew the top sleeve to the under sleeve along both seams. Press the seams open using a tailor's ham or a sleeveboard. Repeat with the other sleeve and the sleeve lining pieces.

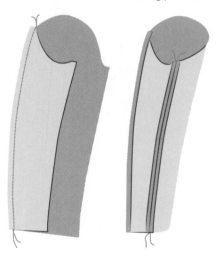

....

TOP TIP

The double notch indicates the back of the sleeve.

....

7 With right sides together, matching the notches, pin the sleeve to the armhole of your coat. Distribute the ease in the sleeve head on either side of the coat's shoulder seam. Sew in place, then trim the armhole seam allowance to 1 cm (⅜ in.) to reduce bulk. Repeat on the coat lining.

8 **Assemble the collar**
Pin and sew the collar pieces right sides together, leaving the inside edge open. Trim the seam allowance down to 5 mm (¼ in.) to reduce bulk.

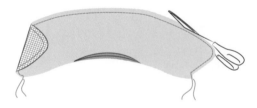

9 Turn the collar right side out and press, using plenty of steam, rolling the seam slightly towards the under collar (the interfaced piece). Use a bamboo pointer to achieve a neat crisp finish on the collar. Machine tack the remaining open edge within the seam allowance.

10 Assemble the facing and collar

If you would like to make a fabric loop to hang up your coat, attach one to the centre of the back facing, on the right side. With right sides together, pin the back facing to the front facings at the shoulder seams. Sew and press the seams open.

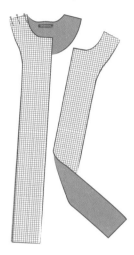

11 Pin the collar to the coat, right sides together and with the interfaced part of the collar underneath, matching the centre back of the collar with the centre back coat seam. Match the notches on the collar to the shoulder seams. Stitch in place. Clip into the seam allowance so that its movement isn't restricted. This will be covered later by the back facing.

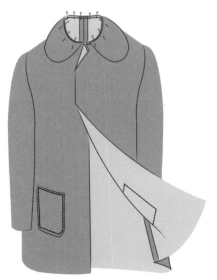

. . . .

TOP TIP

Note that the collar will not meet at the front of the coat.

. . . .

12 With right sides together, matching the notches on the bottom edge of the back facing, pin and sew the coat lining to the facing. Press the seams towards the lining. Clip the curved neckline and understitch to the lining.

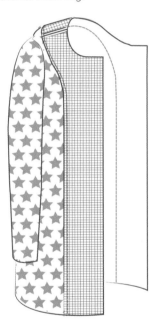

13 Attach the lining

With the facing and lining now in one piece, it's time to attach the entire lining to the coat. With the lining inside out, lay the lining on top of the coat so that right sides are facing each other. Pin the lining to the centre front edges of the coat, right sides together. Also pin the neckline of the lining to the neckline of the coat all the way around, sandwiching the collar in between. Starting at the bottom of one centre front, sew along the centre front, around the neckline, and down the other centre front. Clip the curves and trim any corners. The coat lining is now attached all around the neckline and centre front, and open around the hem and sleeve hem.

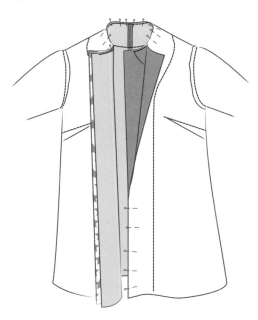

14 Turn the facing and lining through so the coat is now right side out. Push out the corners of the front facing with a bamboo pointer. Separate the lining from the coat at the top of the coat and understitch the collar seam to the coat facing. Press and roll the seams of the coat slightly to the inside of the garment, giving everything a good press.

15 Finish the hems

Press the hem of the sleeve lining to the wrong side by 1.5 cm (⅝ in.). Press the top fabric sleeve up to the wrong side by 4 cm (1½ in.) and herringbone stitch it in place (see page 24). Pin the sleeve lining to the main fabric sleeve and check from the right side to make sure the lining isn't pulling the sleeve up. Slipstitch in place when the lining is in the correct position.

16 Press the hem of the coat lining to the wrong side by 1.5 cm (¾ in.), gradually going to 4 cm (1½ in.) by the time it reaches the front facing, and press the coat hem top fabric up by 4 cm (1½ in.). Herringbone stitch the coat hem allowance in place, just as you did with the sleeves. Pin the lining to the coat around the hem and check from the outside that the lining isn't pulling up the garment. Slipstitch in place.

17 As this is a woman's garment, overlap the wearer's right over left and sew the poppers on by hand. (The pointed half of the popper should be sewn to the inside of the wearer's right and the flat half to the outside of the wearer's left.) Have an odd number of poppers – three or five – and position them as indicated on your pattern.

18 Sew buttons to the front of the coat (on the wearer's right) to correspond with the poppers.

VARIATION

Collarless Coat

Perfect for beginners, this variation takes away the challenge of applying the collar and pockets without compromising on style.

Materials

- ○ Sizes 4–10: 2.2m (2½ yd) fabric 150 cm (60 in.) wide
- ○ Sizes 12–18: 2.6 m (3 yd) fabric 150 cm (60 in.) wide
- ○ Sizes 4–10: 1.6 m (1¾ yd) lining fabric 150 cm (60 in.) wide
- ○ Sizes 12–18: 1.9 m (2 yd) lining fabric 150 cm (60 in.) wide
- ○ 1m (1 yd) interfacing
- ○ 3–5 coat buttons
- ○ 3–5 big poppers

Difficulty level

Confident beginners and improvers

1 Cut out the pieces, omitting the pocket and collar pieces.

2 Omitting steps 5, 8, 9 and 11, make up the coat following the instructions for the Carnaby Coat on pages 106–111.

1 Top sleeve – cut 2

2 Front – cut 2

3 Back – cut 2

4 Front facing – cut 2 in main and 2 in interfacing

5 Under sleeve – cut 2

6 Back facing – cut 1 on the fold in main and 1 on the fold in interfacing

7 Front lining – cut 2

8 Lining top sleeve – cut 2

9 Lining under sleeve – cut 2

10 Back lining - cut 2

150 cm (60 in.) wide fabric

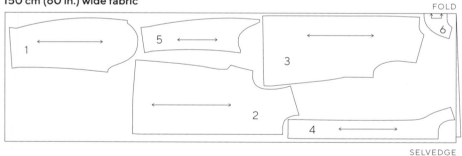

Lining

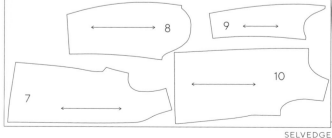

Interfacing

Wiggle Dress

This classic, feminine dress shape has never gone out of fashion since its heyday in the 1960s. It has a fitted shape, created through bust and waist darts in the bodice and matching waist darts in the skirt. This dress fastens with an invisible zip at the back and has a vent in the skirt hem to allow for more movement. The stunning square neckline is faced all around, which makes for an impeccable finish, and the dress has short, pleated cap sleeves. A dress like this is perfect as it works equally well for formal and festive occasions.

TO MAKE THE WIGGLE DRESS

Materials

- Sizes 4–10: 2.6 m (2⅞ yd) fabric 115 cm (45 in.) wide or 1.7 m (1⅞ yd) fabric 150 cm (60 in.) wide
- Sizes 12–18: 2.8 m (3 yd) fabric 115 cm (45 in.) wide or 2.1 m (2¼ yd) fabric 150 cm (60 in.) wide
- 30 cm (12 in.) interfacing
- 61-cm (24-in.) invisible zip
- Basic sewing kit (see page 14)

Difficulty level

Confident beginners and improvers

Fabric suggestions

Choose sturdier fabrics like medium-weight cotton, drill, denim (with some stretch if you like) or cotton satin. Play it safe in darker colours that suit your colouring or go for an all-over print for an eye-catching dress.

Design notes

Use a 1.5-cm (⅝-in.) seam allowance throughout, unless otherwise stated.

Instructions are given for overlocking the seam allowances, but if you don't have an overlocker you can neaten the seam allowances by zigzagging them instead.

Finished measurements	4	6	8	10	12	14	16	18
Front length (cm)	121.5	122	122.5	123	124	124.5	125	125.5
Front length (in.)	47⅞	48	48¼	48½	48¾	49	49¼	49½
Back length (cm)	118	118.5	119.5	120	120.5	121	121.5	122
Back length (in.)	46½	46⅝	47	47¼	47½	47⅝	47⅞	48
Bust (cm)	84.5	89.5	94.5	99.5	104.5	109.5	114.5	119.5
Bust (in.)	33¼	35¼	37¼	39¼	41¼	43⅛	45	47
Waist (cm)	68	73	78	83	88	93	98	103
Waist (in.)	26¾	28¾	30¾	32¾	34¾	36¾	38½	40½
Low hip (cm)	93.5	98.5	103.5	108.5	113.5	118.5	123.5	128.5
Low hip (in.)	36¾	38¾	40¾	42¾	44¾	46¾	48¾	50½
Sleeve length (cm)	14	14.5	15	15.5	16	16.5	17	17.5
Sleeve length (in.)	5½	5¾	6	6⅛	6¼	6½	6¾	6⅞

CUTTING GUIDE

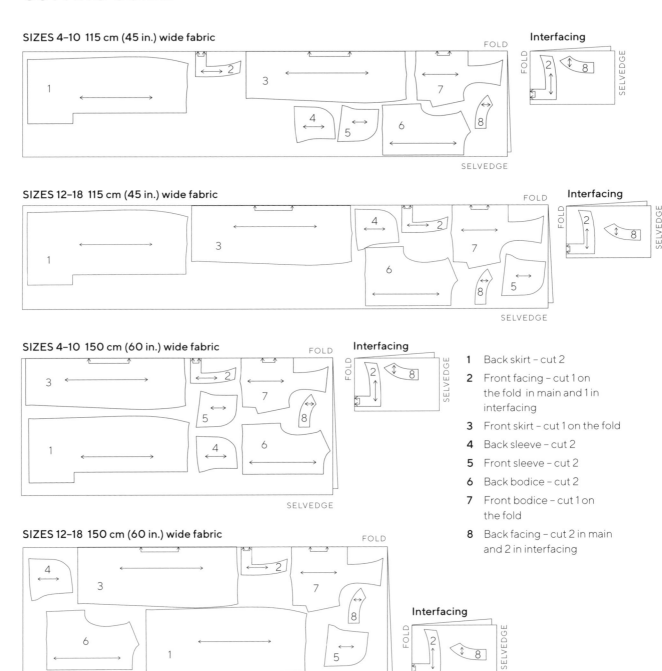

SIZES 4–10 115 cm (45 in.) wide fabric

SIZES 12–18 115 cm (45 in.) wide fabric

SIZES 4–10 150 cm (60 in.) wide fabric

SIZES 12–18 150 cm (60 in.) wide fabric

Interfacing

FOLD

SELVEDGE

1 Back skirt – cut 2

2 Front facing – cut 1 on the fold in main and 1 in interfacing

3 Front skirt – cut 1 on the fold

4 Back sleeve – cut 2

5 Front sleeve – cut 2

6 Back bodice – cut 2

7 Front bodice – cut 1 on the fold

8 Back facing – cut 2 in main and 2 in interfacing

THE SEWING STARTS HERE

1 **Prepare the pieces**
Following the manufacturer's instructions, apply interfacing to the wrong side of the front and back facings.

2 **Insert the darts**
Pin the two darts on the front skirt and sew from the waist to the point. Press the darts towards the side seams.

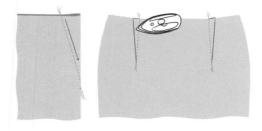

TOP TIP

Don't backstitch at the point of the dart: run off exactly where the dart finishes, leave a tail of thread and tie it off by hand. This way you get a perfect point.

3 Pin and sew the waist darts on the back skirt and press them towards the centre back.

4 Pin and sew the two waist darts and two bust darts on the front. Press the bust darts downwards and the waist darts towards the side seams. It's a good idea to press the darts over a pressing ham (see page 100) so as not to crush the shaping.

TOP TIP

Turn to page 100 for instructions on how to make your own pressing ham.

5 Pin and sew the waist darts in the back bodice and press them towards the centre back.

TOP TIP

To see how to fit darts to your shape, turn to page 33.

6 **Construct the bodice**
Place the front and back bodices right sides together, then pin and sew the side seams. Overlock the seam allowances together at a foot's width and press towards the back.

7 Place the front and back facings right sides together, and pin and sew the shoulder seams. Press the seam allowances open without finishing off the raw edges. Then overlock the entire outside edge of the facings.

8 **Attach the facings**
With right sides together, pin the front and back facings to the bodice. Make sure you pin the shoulders first, so that they match, and match the corners of the neckline. Sew the neckline, starting at the centre back and pivoting at the corners.

TOP TIP

Put plenty of pins along the neckline, as some parts are on the bias and can stretch if you pull the fabric under the machine.

9 Trim the seam allowances to 5 mm (¼ in.). Clip into the front corners of the neckline and the curve of the back neckline at regular intervals.

10 Press the facing to the inside of the bodice, roll it slightly further in with your fingers so that the seam doesn't sit right on the edge, and press. Starting at the centre back, understitch within the facing all around the neckline, using your presser foot as a guide to stitch roughly 3 mm (⅛ in.) away from the neckline seam. This stitch will not be visible on the outside.

TOP TIP

When understitching, have the facing flat on one side and the bodice flat on the other, so that you can easily access the neckline seam with the presser foot.

11 To finish, work a small hand stitch on the inside shoulder to attach the facing to the bodice shoulder seam allowance.

12 **Construct the skirt**
Pin the front and back skirt pieces right sides together, and sew the side seams. Overlock the seam allowances together and press towards the centre back. Leave the centre back seam undone until later. Overlock the centre back edges from the waist to the vent point.

13 **Construct the sleeves**
Place the front and back sleeve piece right sides together, pin and sew along the curve (see page 25). Press the seam allowances open and overlock them separately. Repeat for the second sleeve.

14 Carefully pin the pleats in place, following the notches on the pattern: the bottom one is a single pleat that pleats upwards and at the top is a box pleat, which is created by folding the outside notches towards the pleat centre (see Special Technique, page 124). Stitch the pleats in place from the wrong side by stitching a line that finishes approximately 4 cm (1½ in.) in from the centre seam of the sleeve. Press carefully. Repeat for the second sleeve.

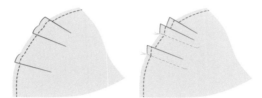

15 Press the sleeve hem up by 1.5 cm (⅝ in.) and then 1.5 cm (⅝ in.) again. Pin the hem and stitch in place as close to the fold as you can.

16 Turn the sleeve right side out and the bodice wrong side out. With right sides together, pin the sleeve into the armhole by matching the centre seam on the sleeve to the shoulder seam on the bodice and the edges of the sleeve armhole to the notches on the bodice. Stitch in place.

17 Overlock the entire armhole at a foot's width and press the armhole seam allowance inwards around the whole armhole. Topstitch around the armhole to hold the seam allowance in place, stitching 5 mm (¼ in.) away from the garment's edge. Repeat for the second sleeve.

18 **Attach the bodice to the skirt**
With right sides together, lay the bodice on top of the skirt so that the raw edges of both waists match; the bodice will be upside down. Pin the skirt and bodice together, matching the waist darts, the side seams and the centre back. Sew the waist seam.

19 Overlock the seam allowances together at a foot's width and press down towards the skirt.

20 Insert an invisible zip from the top of the centre back bodice to the zip notch in the skirt (see page 28). Fold the facing out of the way at the top of the centre back and align the zip teeth with the top of the bodice as best as you can. Tuck the upper ends of the zip tape inside and fold the facing down. Fold the seam allowance of the facing under and slipstitch it to the zip tape.

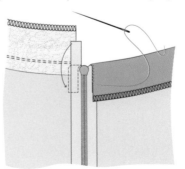

21 Construct the vent

Sew the centre back seam of the skirt from the bottom of the zip seam to the top of the marked vent. Looking at the inside of your skirt, overlock the vent seam allowance on the left skirt (on your left as you look at it) without taking any of the material off, then press the overlocked edge to the wrong side of the skirt and stitch a 1-cm (⅜-in.) hem along the edge of the vent. Now hem the whole skirt (including the vent hem) by turning up a double 1.5-cm (⅝-in.) hem and stitching it in place by hand or by machine.

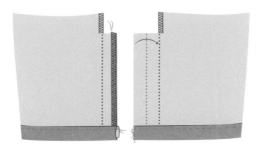

22 Press the right skirt vent to the wrong side along the fold line and then fold again so that the vent is visually in line with the centre back seam. When the two vents are lying on top of each other, they should now be about the same size. Start stitching on the centre back seam 2 cm (¾ in.) above the vent, pivot in the vent corner, then stitch a diagonal line across the top of the vent. Snip into the corner where the vent starts, cutting through both layers, then press the centre back seam allowance open. Finish off the top edge seam allowances of the vent by overlocking them together. Secure the right-hand vent at the hem with a small hand stitch.

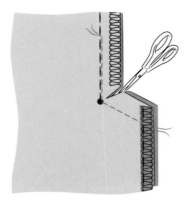

23 Looking at the inside of your dress, press the vent to the right-hand side of the skirt. Turn the dress right side out and work a few stitches diagonally across the top of the vent (by hand or machine) to hold the vent in place.

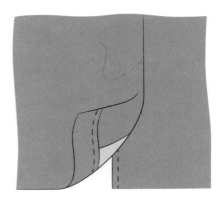

SPECIAL TECHNIQUE: PLEATS

Pleats are a way of adding and controlling volume in a garment. You will often find them around the waist on blouses, dresses, skirts and trousers. The method used determines how much volume you can add.

Knife pleats

Knife pleats are equal folds on the inside and the outside, all facing in the same direction.

Box pleats

Box pleats consist of two knife pleats that face away from each other. The volume sits on the outside of this pleat.

Inverted box pleats

These are the same as box pleats, but in reverse: the two knife pleats face towards each other. The volume sits on the inside of this pleat.

Constructing pleats

1 Pleat lines on your pattern are indicated by two lines and an arrow for the direction in which to fold the pleat. The line that the arrow is pointing to is called the Placement Line; the other line is the Fold Line. Fold the fabric at the Fold Line mark and bring it to the Placement Line mark, keeping the raw edges of the fabric even. The pleat formed will be half the width of the marked fabric.

PATTERN MARKINGS FOR A KNIFE PLEAT

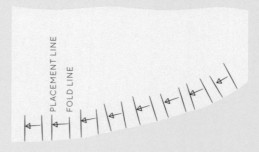

PATTERN MARKINGS FOR A BOX PLEAT

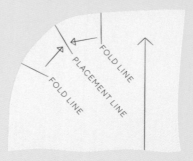

2 For pleats that are functional rather than decorative (like a waist pleat), the pleats are only pinned and pressed right at the edge, so they can be sewn into the seam. We recommend machine tacking them down within the seam allowance. The rest of the pleat creates volume in the garment. Some garments have pleats along the entire length of the garment for decoration and volume (like a pleated skirt), in which case you press the entire pleat to make it lie nice and flat.

3 Machine tack across the top of the pleats to hold them in place, tacking within the seam allowance. You can also stitch down the first few centimetres of the pleat to create a flatter shape, as in the Jumpsuit on page 160. To do this, stitch very close to the folded edge of the pleat.

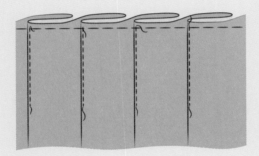

4 To keep pleats folded in place, working from the wrong side, machine stitch close to the inner fold, particularly in the hem area.

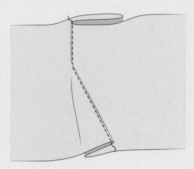

5 Press your pleats very carefully if you are pressing them in! Place a pressing cloth in between the iron and the garment to prevent the pleat indentations showing on the garment.

Scraps Jacket

Just like the mini skirt on page 82, we have used offcuts to create this square-cut open jacket, which you can create in delicate fabrics for a summer garment, or in a sturdier fabric such as denim for a more natural look. You can add ties to the collar or even add a waist tie, or simply embrace the boxy shape.

Materials

- Fabric scraps of a similar weight that go nicely together

- Bias binding for the sleeve hems, neck, centre front and hem

- Plain fabric, such as light cotton, to line the garment (optional)

- Basic sewing kit (see page 14)

1   This garment is made out of three rectangles: one that forms the body and two that form the sleeves. It has no shoulder seam, but the shoulder line would lie halfway through the big rectangle, where the head opening is.

For the body, measure from your nape to the desired length of the garment, and multiply that by two. This will form the length of the large rectangle. The width of the rectangle is roughly 60 cm (24 in.). Add hem allowances. Draw a slightly oval shape in the centre for the head opening.

If you want tie fastenings along the centre front opening, make sure the centre front edges touch (solid line). For an open jacket, separate and shape the centre front lines (red line).

For the sleeves, measure from your shoulder to the desired length for the length. For the width, loosely measure your armhole and use that. If you want a more shaped sleeve, bring the lines in slightly towards the wrist. Add seam allowances.

Cut out your paper pattern pieces.

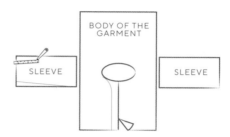

2   Lay out your fabric scraps to get a good distribution of colours and patterns – remember to allow for seam allowances! When you're happy with the arrangement, stitch them together, and press the seams open. Lay the patterns on top of the patchwork and cut out the pieces.

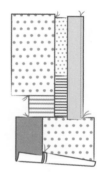

3   With right sides together, pin and sew the sleeves to the centre of the body rectangle. Overlock the seam allowances, then press towards the body.

4   With right sides together, aligning the underarm and side edges, fold your garment in half. Pin and sew the underarm and side seam on each side in one go. Overlock the seam allowances and press towards the back of the garment.

5   Bind the sleeve hems, the neckline, the centre front and the hem (see page 71).

Lining (optional)

Using the same pattern pieces, cut out the lining pieces. Assemble the lining in the same way as the jacket. After step 3, slot the lining into the jacket, with wrong sides together. Machine tack within the seam allowance around the sleeve hems, neck, centre front and hem. Bind these edges to finish (see page 71).

Flared Trousers

These 1970s-inspired flares feature all the classic trouser essentials: a zip fly, belt loops, back pockets and a back yoke. They look amazing with trainers and a dark turtleneck for that easy-going '70s vibe or with a crisp shirt and a belt for a smart-casual work look. The fly construction will test your skills, while finishing the trousers with felled seams will strengthen them and add a technical touch.

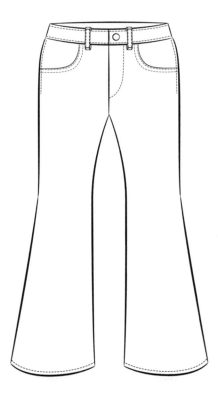

TO MAKE THE FLARED TROUSERS

Materials

- 2.6 m (2⅞ yd) fabric 150 cm (60 in.) wide
- 40 cm (15 in.) calico, cotton or silesia to make the pocket bag
- 30 cm (12 in.) interfacing
- 18-cm (7-in.) closed metal zip
- 1 jeans button
- Basic sewing kit (see page 14)
- Twin needle (optional)

Difficulty level

Improvers

Fabric suggestions

Corduroy, denim, cotton velvet

Design notes

Use a 1.5-cm (⅝-in.) seam allowance throughout, unless otherwise stated.

Instructions are given for overlocking the seam allowances, but if you don't have an overlocker you can neaten the seam allowances by zigzagging them instead.

You can interface the waistband to prevent it from stretching during wear, but if you want a garment that behaves like jeans, leave it out.

Finished measurements	34	36	38	40	42	44
Waistband (cm)	87	92	97	102	107	112
Waistband (in.)	34¼	36¼	38¼	40⅛	42⅛	44
Crotch length (cm)	63	66	69	72	75	78
Crotch length (in.)	24¾	26	27⅛	28⅜	29½	30¾
Inside leg (cm)	85	85	85	85	85	85
Inside leg (in.)	33½	33½	33½	33½	33½	33½

CUTTING GUIDE

150 cm (60 in.) wide fabric

FOLD

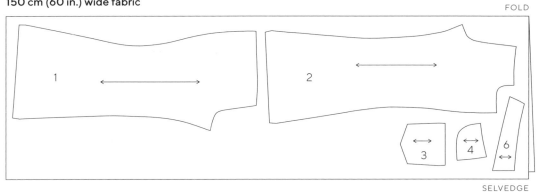

SELVEDGE

150 cm (60 in.) wide fabric

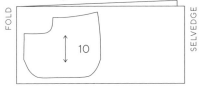

Pocketing

Interfacing

1	Back leg – cut 2
2	Front leg – cut 2
3	Back pocket – cut 2
4	Pocket facing – cut 2
5	Belt loop – cut 5
6	Yoke – cut 2
7	Fly guard – cut 1
8	Fly facing – cut 1 in main and 1 in interfacing
9	Waistband – cut 1
10	Pocket bag – cut 2 in pocketing

THE SEWING STARTS HERE

1 Construct the back pockets

Press a double 1.5-cm (⅝-in.) hem to the wrong side along the top edge of the back pockets and stitch. Press the remaining edges to the wrong side by 1.5 cm (⅝ in.) and pin the pockets on the trouser backs, using plenty of pins. Topstitch in place close to the edge, then topstitch a second line a foot's width inside the first stitching to create a double stitch line.

2 Attach the yokes

With wrong sides together, pin and stitch the yokes to the back leg pieces. From the right side, press the seam allowances and yokes upwards and trim only the yoke seam allowance to half the width. (The seam allowances are supposed to be visible on the right side of the trouser leg.)

3

Fold the trouser seam allowance up and over the trimmed yoke seam allowance to encase all the raw edges; this is known as a felled seam. Topstitch the edge of the felled seam with a normal needle or a twin needle.

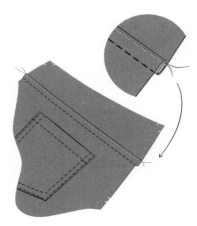

4

Pin the back trousers wrong sides together along the crotch and stitch a felled seam, as in steps 2 and 3, pressing to the left.

TOP TIP

If you are confident about your stitching, why not do the topstitching in a contrasting colour?

5 Construct the front pockets

Work on your pockets as a pair so you don't make two the same: they should mirror each other. Overlock the curved edge of both pocket facings, which are made in the main fabric. Then lay them on top of the pocket bags and topstitch within the seam allowance along all three edges. You should see the right side of the pocket bag as well as the right side of the pocket facing.

6 Place the pocket bags and front trouser legs right sides together, then pin and sew along the curved edge (your pocket opening). Trim the seam allowance and snip into it, then flip the pocket bag to the wrong side of the trouser front. Press along the curved edge so that it sits nicely, then topstitch along the curve with a single or a twin needle.

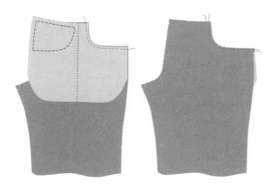

7 Fold the pocket bag in half along the fold line, right sides together. Pin and sew the bottom edge of the pocket bag and overlock at a foot's width. Where the pocket bag meets the side seam, machine tack within the seam allowance so that you can treat the front leg as a whole.

8 Construct the fly zip front

Construct and insert the fly zip (see Special Technique, page 136).

9 Assemble the trousers

With right sides together, place the front trouser on top of the back trouser. Pin and sew the inside legs together. Overlock the seam allowances together at a foot's width and press towards the back. Turn right side out and topstitch both inside leg seams (towards the back).

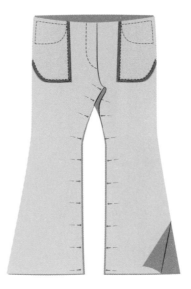

10 With right sides together, pin and sew the side seams. Overlock the seam allowances together at a foot's width and press towards the back. Turn right side out and topstitch from the waist to the bottom of the pocket bag to reinforce the seam and hold everything in place.

11 **Construct the waistband**
Overlock one long edge of each belt loop, then place it wrong side up and fold each long edge in by one third, ending with the overlocked edge on top. Topstitch along both long edges. Pin the loops right sides together to the raw edge of the waist, as indicated by notches on the pattern – one at the centre back, two on each side back, two on each side front. Machine tack in place within the seam allowance.

12 Press under one long edge of the waistband by 1.5 cm (⅝ in.). With right sides together, matching any notches, pin the unpressed long edge of the waistband to the trousers, sandwiching the belt loops in between. Stitch in place. Press the seam allowances and the waistband up.

13 Fold the waistband in half, with right sides together, and sew across the short centre front edges. Trim the seam allowance and turn the waistband right side out.

14 Pin the pressed waistband edge to the trousers by pinning through the waist seam on the outside of the trousers and catching the waistband edge on the inside. Pin all the way around, then stitch in the ditch from the outside (see page 81, step 12).

SPECIAL TECHNIQUE: MAKING A MEN'S FLY ZIP

1 Overlock both front crotch curves on the front trouser pieces. With right sides together, pin the curve from the inside leg seam to the zip notch and sew.

2 Interface the wrong side of the fly facing and overlock the curved edge only; try not to take any fabric off with your overlocker. Pin the fly facing on the right-hand side of the trouser front (as you look at it), right sides together. Pin and sew from the waist to the zip notch.

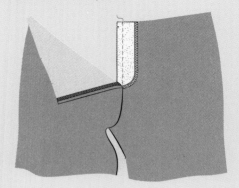

3 Press the facing away from the right trouser leg, then trim the seam allowance and press it away from the trouser leg as well. Place the zip face down on the facing, aligning the bottom of the zip with the zip notch. Align the side of the zip with the seam the joins the facing to the trousers. Sew the left side of the zip to the facing, then fold the facing towards the inside of the trousers and press lightly.

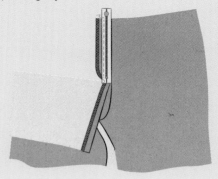

4 Fold the fly guard in half, right sides together. Sew the short curved edge, trim and clip the seam allowance, then turn right side out. Overlock the longest straight edge.

5 Open the zip. Place the trousers right side up, then press 5 mm (¼ in.) to the wrong side on the left-hand side trouser front (as you look at it). Tack the zip in place behind the fold; you should only see the zip teeth. Position the fly guard behind the trousers, aligning the overlocked edge with the edge of the zip tape, and edge stitch close to the trouser front fold through all three layers (trousers, zip and fly guard).

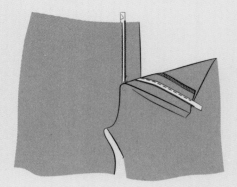

TOP TIP

If you need to cut the zip to create the right length for your garment, hand sew a tack across the top before cutting so that you don't accidentally pull the zip head entirely out of the zip before it's been sewn in.

6 Turn the trousers over so that you can see the inside. Pin the fly guard out of the way to prepare for topstitching. Close the zip and turn the trousers right side up again.

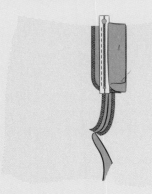

7 Draw a topstitching curve that matches the shape of the fly facing underneath and sew through the trousers and the facing.

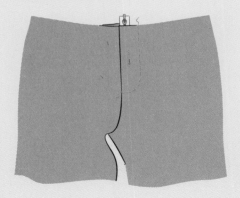

8 Unpin the fly guard so that it sits over the zip. Pin the fly guard in position where it wants to sit. From the front of the trousers, bar tack at the very bottom of the topstitched line and also at the start of the curve. These stitches will go through all layers: trousers, zip, facing and fly guard. Your fly zip is finished! If the zip is too long, trim it above the waist seam allowance.

15 Topstitch along all edges of the waistband. Attach the belt loops to the top edge of the waistband by folding them towards the wrong side by 1 cm (⅜ in.) and working a tiny zigzag stitch backwards and forwards across the top. Secure the bottom edges of the belt loops in the same way.

16 **Finish the trousers**
Turn under a double 1.5-cm (⅝-in.) hem, or create a deeper hem look by turning up 1 cm and then 2 cm (⅜ in. and then ¾ in.). Stitch close to the folded edge.

TOP TIP

These are men's trousers, so just like jackets they will fasten left side over right. Women's trousers have the fly and the button the other way around.

17 Make a horizontal buttonhole on the left-hand side of the waistband and attach a jeans button on the opposite side.

Straight-legged Trousers

If you would like a modern cut to your trousers, use the alternative cutting line on the pattern to make the legs straighter. You can use an array of fabrics for this pattern, including corduroy inspired by the flares worn in the 1970s.

Materials

- 2.6 m (2⅞ yd) fabric 150 cm (60 in.) wide
- 40 cm (15 in.) calico, cotton or silesia to make the pocket bag
- 30 cm (12 in.) interfacing
- 18-cm (7-in.) closed metal zip
- 1 jeans button
- Basic sewing kit (see page 14)
- Twin needle (optional)

Difficulty level

Improvers

1 Cut out the pieces, following the lay plan on page 131 and using the straight cutting line on the front and back leg pattern pieces.

2 Make up the trousers, following the instructions for the Flared Trousers on pages 132–139.

Finished measurements	34	36	38	40	42	44
Waistband (cm)	87	92	97	102	107	112
Waistband (in.)	34¼	36¼	38⅛	40⅛	42⅛	44
Crotch length (cm)	63	66	69	72	75	78
Crotch length (in.)	24¾	26	27⅛	28⅜	29½	30¾
Inside leg (cm)	84.5	84.5	84.5	84.5	84.5	84.5
Inside leg (in.)	33¼	33¼	33¼	33¼	33¼	33¼

Pinafore Skirt

In this project, you will learn how to turn a pair of corduroy jeans into a simple pinafore dress by opening up the inside leg seams and using leg fabric for the pinafore front. There are no set rules, so go with what you have. A shorter skirt will leave you with more material to play with for the top half, but a slightly longer version can make for a more sophisticated look.

Materials

- Pair of full-length jeans
- Basic sewing kit (see page 14)
- Unpicker or sharp small snips
- Denim needle (size 90)

Note: You may need extra fabric for the pinafore straps.

1   Unpick the inside leg seams of the jeans.

2   Decide how long you want your skirt to be, add 3 cm (1¼ in.) for the hem, then trim the jeans legs to this length, making sure you cut off the same amount from each leg. You'll use the cut-off fabric to make the pinafore front.

3   Pin the curved crotch seam down as flat as you can on both the centre front and the centre back and topstitch it in place. Depending on the length of your new skirt, you may find that there's a triangular gap in between what used to be the legs. You can either insert a piece of fabric here or, if it's a small gap, leave it as a little split. We left the button waist closure on as a feature.

4   Overlock the raw bottom edge of the skirt, then turn up and stitch a 3-cm (1¼-in.) hem.

5   Open out one of the pieces of fabric that you cut off the legs and lay it flat; this will be the pinafore front. Cut it to the size you want and hem the sides and the top edge. We also cut the pinafore front down the middle and inserted a new zip down the entire front. Sew the pinafore front to the inside of the skirt waist.

TOP TIP

Watch out for bulky seams when you decide how to fasten your new pinafore!

6   Make straps that cross your back out of leftover fabric or anything else you like, and stitch them to the top of the front and the back waistband.

Maxi Dress

With its many tiered skirts, this full-length maxi dress is the perfect pattern to mix and match prints, colours and fabrics. Wear it to the market on a Sunday with sneakers or with heels for an event.

TO MAKE THE MAXI DRESS

Materials

- Sizes 4–10: 3.5 m (4 yd) fabric 150 cm (60 in.) wide
- Sizes 12–18: 4 m (4½ yd) fabric 150 cm (60 in.) wide
- 40 cm (16 in.) interfacing
- 55-cm (21½-in.) invisible zip
- 2 cuff buttons
- 3-5 front buttons (optional)

Difficulty level

Improvers

Fabric suggestions

We suggest using fabrics with plenty of movement and drape, such as viscose/rayon, bamboo silk, tencel, crepe, cotton lawn chambray, silk double gauze, crepe de chine, light linen or georgette.

Design notes

Use a 1.5-cm (⅝-in.) seam allowance throughout, unless otherwise stated.

Instructions are given for overlocking the seam allowances, but if you don't have an overlocker you can neaten the seam allowances by zigzagging them instead.

Finished measurements	4	6	8	10	12	14	16	18
Front length (cm)	151	151.5	152.5	153	153.5	154	154.5	155.5
Front length (in.)	59½	59⅝	60	60¼	60½	60⅝	60⅞	61¼
Back length (cm)	149	149.5	150	150.5	151.5	153	152.5	153
Back length (in.)	58⅝	58⅞	59	59¼	59⅝	60¼	60	60¼
Bust (cm)	101	106	111	116	121	126	131	136
Bust (in.)	39¾	41¾	43¾	45⅝	47⅝	49⅝	51½	53½
Waist (cm)	68.5	73.5	78.5	83.5	88.5	93.5	98.5	103.5
Waist (in.)	27	29	31	32⅞	34⅞	36¾	38¾	40¾
Sleeve length (cm)	31.5	32	32.5	33	33.5	34	34.5	35
Sleeve length (in.)	12⅜	12½	12¾	13	13⅛	13⅜	13½	13¾

CUTTING GUIDE

SIZES 4–10 150 cm (60 in.) wide fabric

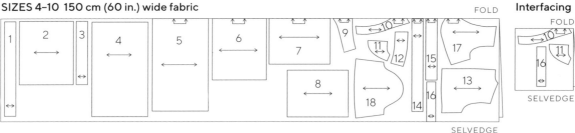

Interfacing

SIZES 12–18 150 cm (60 in.) wide fabric

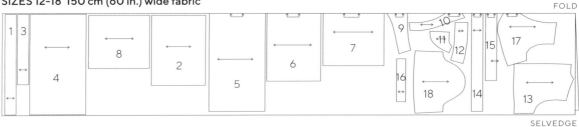

Interfacing

1   Tier 2 frill back – cut 2
2   Tier 2 back skirt – cut 2
3   Tier 1 frill back – cut 2
4   Tier 3 back skirt – cut 2
5   Tier 3 front skirt – cut 1 on the fold
6   Tier 2 front skirt – cut 1 on the fold
7   Tier 1 front skirt – cut 1 on the fold
8   Tier 1 back skirt – cut 2
9   Front waistband – cut 1 on the fold
10 Front facing – cut 1 on the fold in main and 1 in interfacing

11 Back facing – cut 2 in main and 2 in interfacing
12 Back waistband – cut 2
13 Back bodice – cut 2
14 Tier 2 frill front – cut 1 on the fold
15 Tier 1 frill front – cut 1 on the fold
16 Cuff – cut 2 in main and 2 in interfacing
17 Front bodice – cut 1 on the fold
18 Sleeve – cut 2

THE SEWING STARTS HERE

1 Prepare the pieces

Following the manufacturer's instructions, apply interfacing to the wrong side of the cuffs and the front and back facings.

2 Stay stitch the V-neckline on the front bodice and the top curved edge of the front waistband, 1 cm (⅜ in.) away from the raw edge. Run two lines of gathering stitches along each side of the bottom edge of the front bodice, in between the notches (under the bust). Use the biggest stitch on your machine (don't backstitch) and stitch one line on top of the pattern line and one line a foot's width into the seam allowance.

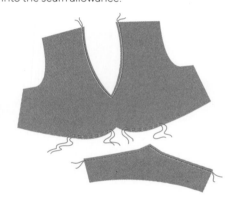

3 Assemble the bodice

With right sides together, matching the notches, lay the front waistband on top of the front bodice. Make a small snip into the V-shaped point of the bodice to be able to sew the pieces together neatly. Distribute the under-bust gathers evenly. Put in plenty of pins in to keep the curve under control and sew, pivoting at the centre point of the waistband. Overlock the seam allowances together at a foot's width, then press the seam down towards the bottom of the bodice.

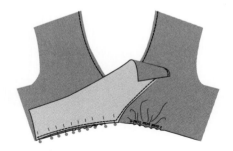

4 Sew two lines of gathering stitches on each of the back bodice pieces, in between the notches, as in step 2. With right sides together, matching the top edge of the waistband with the bottom edge of the bodice, lay the waistband back pieces on the bodice back pieces. Draw up the gathers evenly, so that the notches on the waistband and bodice match. Pin in place, then sew. Overlock the seam allowances together at a foot's width, then press the seam down towards the bottom of the bodice.

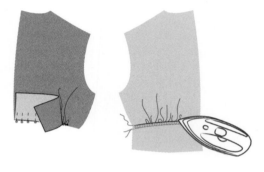

5 With right sides together, pin and sew the front bodice and back bodices together along the shoulder and side seams. Press the shoulder seams open and overlock the seam allowances separately. Overlock the side seams together at a foot's width and press the seams towards the back bodice pieces.

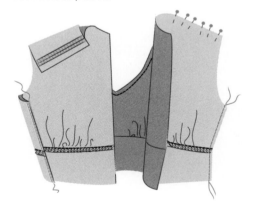

6 Construct the sleeves
Sew two lines of gathering stitches along the cuff edge of the sleeve, starting and finishing 1.5 cm (⅝in.) from each end. With right sides together, pin and sew the underarm sleeve seam. Press the seam open and overlock the seam allowances separately. Repeat on the other sleeve.

7 With right sides together, pin and sew the cuff edges together along the short sides. Press the seam allowances open. Press the seam allowance on one edge to the wrong side of the cuff, using plenty of steam. Then fold the cuff in half lengthwise, with wrong sides together, and press the fold line in to create a crease.

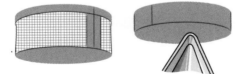

8 Distribute the gathers along the bottom edge of the sleeve. Unfold the central crease in the cuff that you made in step 7. With right sides together, matching the seams, pin the unpressed side of the cuff to the sleeve edge. Stitch, then trim the seam allowance down to 1 cm (⅜ in.) to reduce bulk. Press the seam down towards the cuff.

9 Turn the cuff to the inside of the sleeve along the pressed crease line to reveal the right side of the cuff and press the crease line again. Slipstitch the pressed seam allowance to cover the inside seam allowance for a neat finish, or stitch in the ditch from the outside (see page 81, step 12).

10 With right sides together, matching the notches, pin then sew the sleeve into the armhole. Overlock the seam allowances together at a foot's width and press the seam towards the bodice. Repeat with the second sleeve.

11 Assemble the skirt
With right sides together, pin and then sew the side seams of the 1st tier front skirt to the 1st tier back skirts. Overlock the seam allowances together, then press the seams towards the back. Repeat with the 2nd and 3rd tier skirt pieces. Sew two lines of gathering stitches along the top of each tier, as in step 2.

12 Pull the gathers on the top of the 2nd tier skirt, making sure they are even all the way around. With right sides together, aligning the side seams and notches, pin the top of the 2nd tier to the bottom of the 1st tier. (The 2nd tier will be lying upside down.) Sew, overlock the seam allowances together at a foot's width and press the seam down towards the skirt.

13 Repeat step 12 to attach the 3rd tier to the 2nd tier, then hem the skirt with a double 1.5-cm (⅝-in.) hem.

14 Optional skirt frills
With right sides together, pin the tier 1 frill back strips to the frill front strip along the short edges to create one long strip. Sew and press the seams open. Overlock the seam allowances separately. Hem both long sides of the frill by turning a double 1-cm (⅜-in.) hem to the wrong side. Make the tier 2 frill in the same way. Sew a line of gathering stitches down the centre of the frills.

15 Pin the frills over the seams between the 1st and 2nd, and 2nd and 3rd tiers. Align the side seams and centre back edges. Distribute the gathers in the frill(s) evenly and stitch on top of the gathering stitches.

16 Sew the skirt to the bodice
Pull the gathers on the 1st tier skirt, making sure the gathering is even all the way around. With right sides together, matching the notches, pin the top of the 1st tier to the bodice. Sew in place and overlock the seam allowances together at a foot's width. Press the seam down towards the skirt, making sure you don't flatten the gathers.

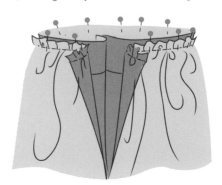

17 Overlock the whole length of both centre back edges of your dress. Starting at the zip notch in the skirt, sew the centre back seam from the zip notch down to the hem. Press the seam open.

18 Insert an invisible zip in the centre back (see page 28), making sure that the top of the zip (where the teeth begin) is 1.5 cm (⅝ in.) below the raw edge of the neckline.

19 Assemble the facing
With right sides together, pin and sew the front facing to the back facings along the shoulder seams. Press the seams open and overlock the seam allowances separately. Overlock the entire outer edge of the facing.

20 With right sides together, aligning the shoulder seams, pin and sew the facing to the neckline of the dress. You will have to pivot carefully at the V-point at the centre front. Clip into the neck curve and the V at the centre front. Trim the seam allowance to 5 mm (¼ in.) to reduce bulk.

21 Turn the facing to the inside of the dress. Understitch the facing so that it stays neatly inside the dress.

22 Fold in the centre back edges of the facing along the zip and sew in place by hand.

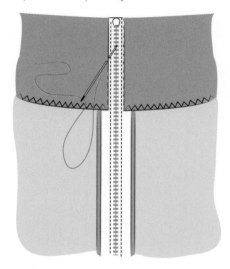

23 Slipstitch the bottom of the front facing to the inside of the dress at the waistband, so that it stays in place. Also hand stitch the facing to the garment's shoulder seam to keep it neatly inside the dress.

24 Add decorative buttons (optional)
For the final touch, position 3–5 buttons along the centre front, making sure they are evenly spaced, and sew on by hand. Hand stitch one button to each cuff.

Midi Dress

Designed for a more casual look, this midi variation is perfect paired with heels, for a more sophisticated occasion, or with tights in winter. Suitable for all body types and heights, it ends just below your calf for a flattering flutter.

Materials

- 3 m (3¼ yd) fabric 150 cm (60 in.) wide
- 40 cm (16 in.) interfacing
- 55-cm (20-in.) invisible zip
- 2 cuff buttons
- 3–5 front buttons (optional)
- Basic sewing kit (see page 14)

Difficulty level

Confident beginners and improvers

1 Cut out the pieces, omitting tier 3 front and back skirt pieces and tier 2 frill piece.

2 Make up the dress, following the instructions for the Maxi Dress on pages 148–152.

150 cm (60 in.) wide fabric

Interfacing

1 Tier 1 frill back – cut 2

2 Tier 1 back skirt – cut 2

3 Tier 2 back skirt – cut 2

4 Tier 2 front skirt – cut 1 on the fold

5 Tier 1 front skirt – cut 1 on the fold

6 Front waistband – cut 1 on the fold

7 Cuff – cut 2 in main and interfacing

8 Front facing – cut 1 on the fold in main and1 in interfacing

9 Back facing – cut 2 in main and 2 in interfacing

10 Back bodice – cut 2

11 Back waistband – cut 2

12 Tier 1 frill front – cut 1 on the fold

13 Sleeve – cut 2

14 Front bodice – cut 1 on the fold

LAUNDRY & DRY CLEANING

When you have made your new clothes, another important step towards a more sustainable wardrobe is how you care for them. The resources used to make clothes are impactful, but how you take care of them for years to come has a similar, if not bigger, impact.

The first thing to think about is how often you wash and at how many degrees. Clothes last longer if they are washed at 20–40° C and this is a more environmentally friendly way to wash than a hotter wash, which you can reserve for bed linens and towels if really necessary. Clothes actually respond better to these washing cycles, as hotter temperatures usually damage the fibres and therefore shorten the lifespan of your garments. Make sure that you wash a full load to make full use of the water.

Sometimes it's only parts of a garment that really need cleaning, so you could consider spot cleaning or a hand wash. If you are washing a garment because it has a stain on it, it's much better to spot clean than to wash the entire garment. Spot cleaning has fallen out of favour a little bit in recent years, but it deserves mention here as a way of reducing the impact our clothes have on the environment, in a way that is completely within our control.

Use a detergent that has a reduced amount of chemicals in it, which includes synthetic fragrances. These detergents are less harmful to the planet's waterways and are a relatively easy way to reduce your laundry's impact. You can also consider making your own. Asking the older generation is usually a great way to find out about effective stain removers and laundry tricks. There are also some great tips online.

Garments made from synthetic fibres, such as polyester, nylon and fleece, contain micro plastics. These are very small particles that are released when submerged in water during a laundry cycle and are washed out into the waterways with the wastewater from the washing machine. There are currently only a limited number of ways to catch these microfibres to keep them out of seas, rivers and oceans, but they do exist. In the near future, there will hopefully be many more solutions.

After you have done your laundry, consider air drying rather than tumble drying to conserve energy.

If you have to dry clean your clothes, look for a dry-cleaning company that eliminates the use of a chemical called percholorethylene, which is the most harmful of all the chemicals used in dry cleaning. There are many alternatives, so look for a dry cleaner near you with greener credentials.

Getting rid of stains

Blood	Dab with saliva, or soak in cold salt water, then dab with ammonia and water.
Sweat	Mix lemon juice, water and salt to scrub the stain before washing.
Lipstick	Scrape off excess, then use a biodegradable baby wipe.
Make-up	Spot treat with washing-up liquid before washing.
Red wine	White wine, or dab with fizzy water, then cover with salt and leave to sit overnight before washing.
Grass	Treat with vinegar before washing.
Ink	Soak in milk before washing.
Oil	Spot clean with white chalk to soak up the moisture.
Coffee and tea	Dab with bicarbonate of soda or white vinegar before washing.
Chocolate	Scrape off excess, spot treat with washing-up liquid before washing.

Dress Bag

Now that you have put so much love and care into making your beautiful garments, why not add a garment bag to your wardrobe so that you can store your clothes between seasons or to protect more delicate items from dust and damage.

This dress bag is made out of hand-embroidered bed linen, passed down through the generations but not used for years. This is a beautiful and practical way to make use of them and extend the life of your own wardrobe at the same time.

Materials

- Vintage linen, such as an embroidered sheet (we used one single sheet)
- 1 m (1 yd) of cotton tape
- Paper for pattern
- Pencil and ruler
- Basic sewing kit (see page 14)

1 On paper, draw a rectangle roughly 120 cm (48 in.) long by 60 cm (24 in.) wide. Draw across the rectangle 30 cm (12 in.) from one short end. Curve the edges of the top section, then cut the pattern into two. Using the pattern pieces, cut two top sections and two main parts from your chosen fabric.

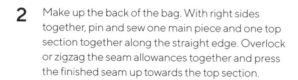

2 Make up the back of the bag. With right sides together, pin and sew one main piece and one top section together along the straight edge. Overlock or zigzag the seam allowances together and press the finished seam up towards the top section.

3 Cut the remaining main part in half lengthwise. Stitch a double 1.5-cm (⅝-in.) hem on each side of the centre cut; this will form the opening. Then sew the remaining curved top to this piece along the straight edges, just as you did for the back; there'll be a gap in the middle of the main part. Overlock or zigzag the seam allowances together and press the finished seam.

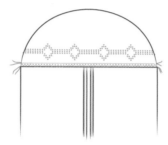

4 Pin the front and back right sides together, aligning the raw edges. If you wish, fold a 15-cm (6-in.) length of cotton tape in half to make a loop and sandwich it in the bottom hem so that, when the bag is finished, you can hook the bottom of the bag over the hanger. Sew all the way around, leaving a gap at the top for the hanger.

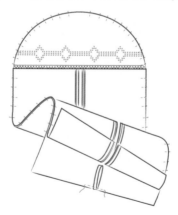

5 Turn the bag right side out. Sew pairs of cotton tapes to the front opening to tie the bag shut.

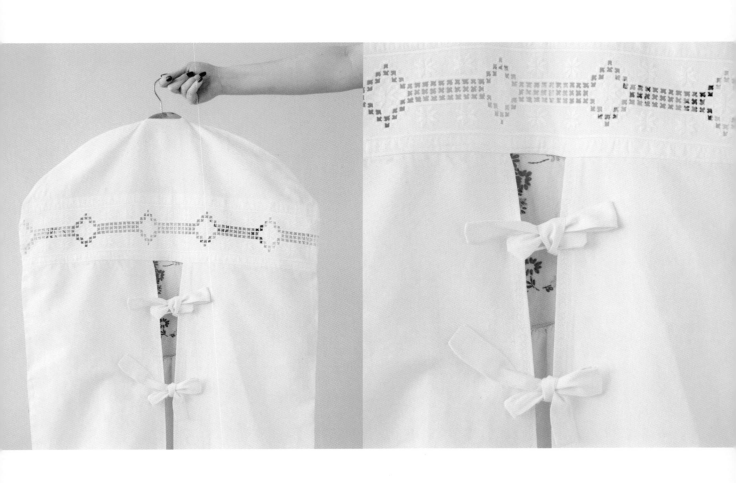

Jumpsuit

A jumpsuit is a perfect all-season staple and a great item to
have in your wardrobe. Sew it up in denim for a weekend look
or bamboo silk for a more dressed-up feel. Featuring a tie waist
that gives you the option of either a nipped-in or a relaxed fit,
additional details such as applied pockets and sleeve tabs gives
this design a boiler-suit finish. This pattern is all about fit and
finishes, so take your time to fit the garment and don't rush
any of the details.

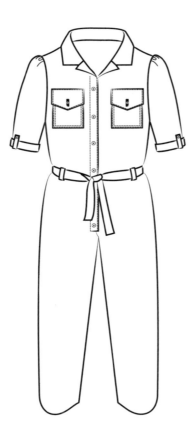

TO MAKE THE JUMPSUIT

Materials

- Sizes 4–10: 3.2 m (3½ yd) fabric 150 cm (60 in.) wide
- Sizes 12–18: 3.9 m (4¼ yd) fabric 150 cm (60 in.) wide
- 20 cm (8 in.) interfacing
- 7 medium buttons for the front fastenings
- 2 pocket buttons
- 2 cuff buttons
- Basic sewing kit (see page 14)

Difficulty level

Improvers

Fabric suggestions

Linen, denim, corduroy, lawn, crepe, suiting or light wool

Design notes

Use a 1.5-cm (⅝-in.) seam allowance throughout, unless otherwise stated.

Instructions are given for overlocking the seam allowances, but if you don't have an overlocker you can neaten the seam allowances by zigzagging them instead.

Finished measurements	4	6	8	10	12	14	16	18
Across front (cm)	35.5	36.5	38	39	40	41.5	42.5	44
Across front (in.)	14	14⅜	15	15⅜	15¾	16⅜	16¾	17⅜
Across back (cm)	37	38	39.5	40.5	42	43	44	45.5
Across back (in.)	14½	15	15½	16	16½	17	17⅜	18
Bust (cm)	100	105	110	115	120	125	130	135
Bust (in.)	39⅜	41⅜	43⅜	45¼	47¼	49¼	51⅛	53⅛
Waist (cm)	77.5	82.5	87.5	92.5	97.5	102.5	107.5	112.5
Waist (in.)	30½	32½	34½	36½	38⅜	40⅜	42⅜	44¼
Sleeve length (cm)	44.5	45	45.5	46	46.5	47	47.5	48
Sleeve length (in.)	17½	17¾	18	18⅛	18⅜	18½	18¾	19
Inside leg (cm)	68.5	68.5	68.5	68.5	68.5	68.5	68.5	68.5
Inside leg (in.)	27	27	27	27	27	27	27	27
Outside leg (cm)	100	100	100	100	100	100	100	100
Outside leg (in.)	39⅜	39⅜	39⅜	39⅜	39⅜	39⅜	39⅜	39⅜

CUTTING GUIDE

SIZES 4–10 150 cm (60 in.) wide fabric

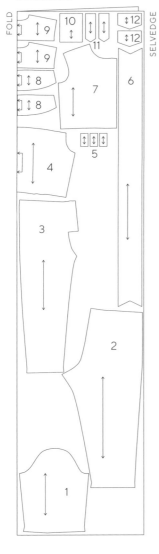

SIZES 12–18 150 cm (60 in.) wide fabric

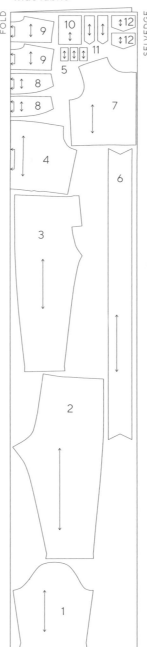

Interfacing

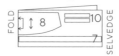

1   Sleeve – cut 2

2   Trouser back – cut 2

3   Trouser front – cut 2

4   Back bodice – cut 1 on the fold

5   Belt loop – cut 5

6   Waistband – cut 1

7   Front bodice – cut 2 in main and 2 strips in interfacing

8   Collar – cut 2 on the fold in main and 1 on the fold in interfacing

9   Yoke – cut 2 on the fold

10 Pocket – cut 2 in main and 2 strips in interfacing

11 Sleeve tab – cut 4

12 Pocket flap – cut 4

THE SEWING STARTS HERE

1 Prepare the pieces
Following the manufacturer's instructions, apply interfacing to one collar piece; this will become the under collar. Apply a 2-cm (¾-in.) wide strip of interfacing along the top edges of the pockets, 1 cm (⅜ in.) away from the raw top edge, and a 3-cm (1¼-in.) wide strip of interfacing down each side of the centre front opening on the bodice and the trousers (right on the centre front edge).

2 Prepare the pockets
Along the top edge of the pockets, press 1 cm (⅜ in.) to the wrong side, then press under the interfaced 2 cm (¾ in.) to create a strong top edge. Topstitch in place. Press 1.5 cm (⅝ in.) to the wrong side all around the sides and bottom edge. Referring to the pattern for the placement, pin the pockets to the front bodice pieces and topstitch in place close to the edge. You can topstitch a second line a foot's width inside the first to create a double stitch line for extra strength.

3 Pin two pocket flap pieces right sides together, then sew along the short sides and the V-shape. Trim the seam allowance and clip into the corners. Turn right side out and use a bamboo pointer to get neat corners. Press well. Overlock the remaining open edges together. You can topstitch along the edges of the pocket flap for a neat effect. Make a vertical buttonhole close to the point of the V-shape. Repeat with the remaining pocket flap pieces.

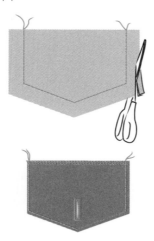

4 Place the pocket flap upside down above the pocket, with the overlocked edge about 1 cm (⅜ in.) away from the pocket's top edge. Sew along the overlocked edge with a regular seam allowance, then press the flap down into its correct position and topstitch 5 mm (¼ in.) away from the top edge to hold the flap down. Mark where the buttonhole hits the pocket and attach a button.

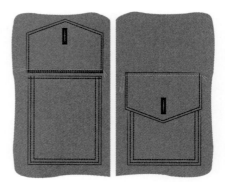

5 Assemble the back bodice and yoke
Looking at the wrong side of the bodice back, fold and pin two box pleats in the back waist (see Special Technique, page 124). Machine tack within the seam allowance to hold them in place.

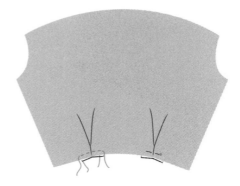

6 Run two lines of gathering stitches across the top of the back blouse, in between the notches. Use the biggest stitch on your machine (don't backstitch) and stitch one line on top of the pattern line and one line a foot's width into the seam allowance.

7 Sandwich the back of the blouse in between the two yokes, with the yokes right sides together. (The yokes will be upside down.) Match the gathering notches on the yoke to the gathering notches on the back of the blouse and then gather up the back of the blouse to fit in between. Put plenty of pins in this area to keep the gathers nice and tidy. Pin along the rest of the seam and sew. Grade the seam allowances to 5 mm–1 cm (¼–½ in.) to eliminate bulk.

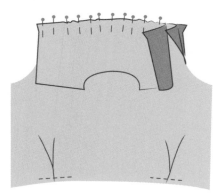

8 Press the yokes upwards, then topstitch from the right side of the garment, 5 mm (¼ in.) away from the seam and towards the yoke.

9 Machine tack the two yokes together around the neckline, shoulders and armholes, stitching within the seam allowance. Your back bodice is now in one piece.

10 **Join the front and back together**
With right sides together, pin and sew the front and back bodices together at the shoulder seams. Overlock the seam allowances together at a foot's width. Press towards the back. From the right side of the garment, topstitch 5 mm (¼ in.) away from the seam, towards the back bodice.

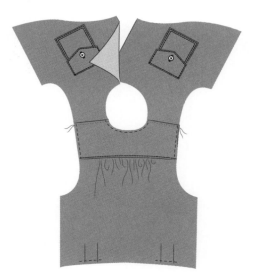

11 **Assemble the collar**
On the non-interfaced collar piece, press 1.5 cm (⅝ in.) to the wrong side along the inner edge (indicated on your pattern). This piece will be the top collar. With right sides together, pin the two collar pieces together. Stitch along all sides except the inner edge; the pressed edge will get caught when you sew the short edges of the collar. Trim the corners of the seam allowance. Also trim the rest of the seam allowance to about 5 mm (¼ in.).

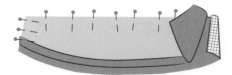

12 Assemble the sleeves

Pin two sleeve tab pieces right sides together and sew along the two vertical edges and the point. Trim the seam allowance to 5 mm (¼ in.) and snip away the seam allowance at the corners. Turn the tab right side out, using a bamboo pointer to get crisp corners. Overlock the remaining open edge. Make a vertical buttonhole, as indicated on your pattern. Repeat with the remaining sleeve tab pieces.

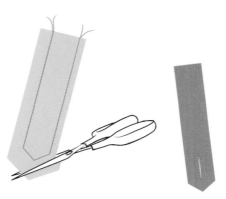

13 Place the tabs on the inside of the sleeves, following the pattern for positioning. As with the pocket flaps, position the tabs upside down and sew along the short edge with a 1.5-cm (⅝-in.) seam allowance. Then press the tab down and topstitch 5 mm (¼ in.) away from the folded edge. On the outside of the sleeves, sew on a button as indicated on the pattern.

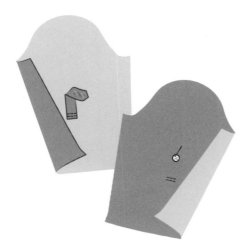

14 Run two lines of gathering stitches across the sleeve heads, in between the notches as indicated on your pattern. With the bodice and sleeves right sides together, matching any notches, pin the sleeves into the armholes and gather the sleeve heads. Sew in place, then overlock the seam allowances together at a foot's width and press towards the bodice.

TOP TIP

A double notch on a sleeve or trouser piece indicates the back and a single notch indicates the front. This way you can double check you are putting the correct sleeve into each armhole.

15 Fold the bodice in half, with right sides together, matching the underarm and side edges. Pin and sew the underarm and side seam on each side all in one. Overlock the seam allowances together at a foot's width and press towards the back.

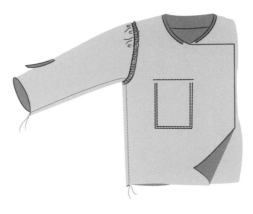

16 Hem the sleeves with a double 1.5-cm (⅝-in.) hem.

17 Construct the trousers
Looking at the wrong side of the back trouser pieces, fold and pin a box pleat in each leg (see Special Technique, page 124). Turn the trouser pieces right side out. Starting from the waist edge, topstitch down each folded edge of the box pleats for 5.5 cm (2 in.).

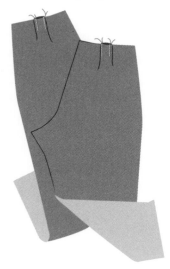

18 Place one trouser front and one trouser back right sides together. Pin and sew the side seam and inside leg seam. Overlock the seam allowances together at a foot's width and press towards the back. Repeat with the remaining trouser front and back pieces.

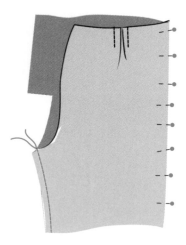

19 Turn one trouser leg right side out and leave the other one wrong side out. Matching the inner leg seams and the notches along the curve, slide one leg inside the other so the right sides are together. Pin and sew the crotch seam up to the start of the button stand in the front crotch. Overlock the seam allowances together at a foot's width (start at the back waist and stop at the notch). Turn the trousers right side out.

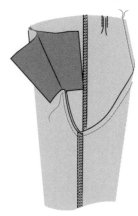

20 Finish the jumpsuit
With right sides together, lay the bodice on top of the trousers so that the raw edges of both waists match; the bodice will be upside down. Pin the bodice and trousers together, matching the side seams, the centre front and the back box pleats. Sew in place. Overlock the seam allowances together at a foot's width and press down towards the trousers.

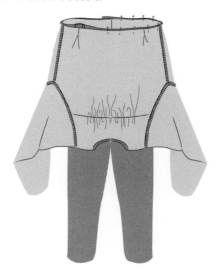

21 Turn the collar right side out, using a bamboo pointer to get crisp corners, and press really well from the side of the under collar, rolling the collar slightly towards the underneath, so that the seam isn't visible from the top collar.

22 Pin the collar to the back neckline of the bodice, with the under collar against the right side of the back. Match the notch on the collar to the shoulder seam and match the front edge of the collar to the notches in the front bodice neckline. Sew only the under collar to the neckline: start from the centre back and sew to one front edge, then start again at the centre back and sew to the opposite centre front edge. Clip into the seam allowance and press it up into the collar.

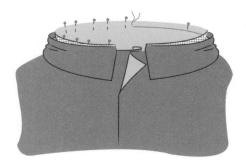

23 Slipstitch the pressed-under open edge of the top collar so that it covers the seam seam allowances, or stitch in the ditch from the right side of the garment (see page 81, step 12).

24 Create the button stands at the centre front. Fold the centre front edge over to the right side of the garment by 6 cm (2½ in.), then fold the raw edge back again towards the centre front by 3 cm (1¼ in.). You should now see the right side of the button stand. Sew across the folded top edge at the neckline with a normal seam allowance until you reach the collar notch. Snip into the corner of the seam allowance. Overlock the bottom of the button stand across the bottom of the centre front edge.

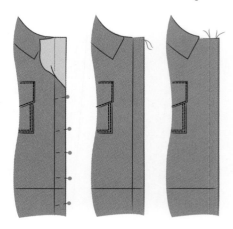

25 Trim the seam allowance, then turn the button stand inside out, so that it ends up on the inside of the garment. Press the button stand, pin it in place, then topstitch along both the centre front edge and the folded edge. Do the same for both centre front edges of your jumpsuit. Machine tack the button stand in place across the bottom edge to keep it in place.

TOP TIP

You will see on your pattern that the centre front line lies in the middle of the button stand. That's the line along which you should position the buttons and buttonholes. See Special Technique, page 185.

26 As this is a woman's garment, the buttons will go on the wearer's left and the vertical buttonholes on the wearer's right. If you want to be able to button the jumpsuit all the way up, use seven buttons: position one right at the top of the button stand, one at the fullest part of the bust, one at the waist, and the others equally in between. If you want to omit the top buttons and roll the lapel out, use five buttons: position one at the point where you want the lapel to stop opening (this is called the breakpoint), one at the waist, and the rest equally in between. Make vertical buttonholes on the wearer's right button stand.

TOP TIP

If you are buttoning the jumpsuit all the way up, make the top buttonhole a horizontal one to allow for more movement and comfort.

27 Make five belt loops (see steps 11 and 15, pages 134 and 139). Position one on each side front, one on each side back and one at the centre back as per the indications on your pattern. Make sure the belt loops sit centrally over the waist seam.

28 With right sides together, fold the belt in half and sew around the majority of the outside edge, leaving a gap so you can turn it right side out. Trim the seam allowances, turn right side out and make crisp corners with a bamboo pointer. Press the seam allowance along the gap to the inside, press the belt really well and topstitch the gap shut. You can also topstitch all the way around the belt.

29 Hem the trousers by turning up 1 cm and then 2 cm (⅜ in. and then ¾ in.) to the inside of the trousers. Sew all around close to the folded edge.

Cropped Jumpsuit

Perfect for sunny breaks, this classic piece will take you from day to night; pair it with chunky wedges for summer strolls and a clutch bag for an evening out. Take your time with this garment and enjoy sewing the many details.

Materials

- Sizes 4–10: 2.5 m (2¾ yd) fabric 150 cm (60 in.) wide
- Sizes 12–18: 2.9 m (3¼ yd) fabric 150 cm (60 in.) wide
- 20 cm (8 in.) interfacing
- 7 medium buttons for the front fastenings
- 2 pocket buttons
- 2 cuff buttons
- Basic sewing kit (see page 14)

For details of how many of each piece to cut, refer to the cutting guide on page 163.

Difficulty level

Improvers

Finished measurements	All sizes
Inside leg cropped (cm)	18.5
Inside leg cropped (in.)	7¼
Outside leg cropped (cm)	50
Outside leg cropped (in.)	20

1 Cut out the pieces, using the shorter cutting line on the front and back leg pattern pieces.

2 Make up the jumpsuit, following the instructions for the full-length version on pages 164–171. .

SIZES 4–10 150 cm (60 in.) wide fabric

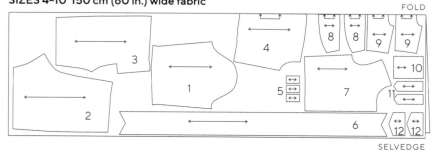

Interfacing

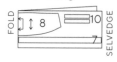

SIZES 12–18 150 cm (60 in.) wide fabric

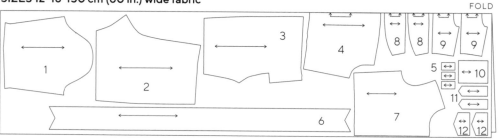

Linen Jacket

This linen jacket, inspired by the style of French workers' jackets from the 1800s, is a beautiful menswear staple that will never go out of fashion. It's unlined and has deep pockets on the front, making it much more practical than a formal jacket. It's perfect for a whole range of occasions, from summer weddings to casual Fridays at work. We used linen, which is made from flax – a very sustainable crop that, unlike many other fibres, is grown in countries across Europe.

TO MAKE THE LINEN JACKET

Materials

- 2.8m (3 yd) fabric 150 cm (60 in.) wide
- 90 cm (1 yd) interfacing
- 3 jacket buttons, 2.5–3.5 cm (1–1⅜ in.)
- Bias binding to cover the inside seam allowances (optional)
- Basic sewing kit (see page 14)

Difficulty level

Improvers

Fabric suggestions

Medium-weight cotton, lightweight denim, linen

Design notes

Use a 1.5-cm (⅝-in.) seam allowance throughout, unless otherwise stated.

Instructions are given for overlocking the seam allowances, but if you don't have an overlocker you can neaten the seam allowances by zigzagging them instead.

Finished measurements	34	36	38	40	42	44
Front length (cm)	74.5	75	76	76.5	77	77.5
Front length (in.)	29¼	29½	30	30⅛	30⅜	30½
Back length (cm)	74.5	75	75.5	76.5	77	77.5
Back length (in.)	29¼	29½	30	30⅛	30⅜	30½
Across back (cm)	43	44.5	45.5	47	48	49
Across back (in.)	17	17½	18	18½	19	19¼
Chest (cm)	109	114	119	124	129	134
Chest (in.)	43	45	47	49	51	53
Waist (cm)	107	112	117	122	127	132
Waist (in.)	42	44	46	48	50	52
Sleeve length (cm)	63.5	64	64.5	65	65.5	66
Sleeve length (in.)	25	25¼	25⅜	25½	25¾	26
Shoulder length (cm)	15	15	15.5	16	16	16.5
Shoulder length (in.)	6	6	6⅛	6¼	6¼	6½

CUTTING GUIDE

150 cm (60 in.) wide fabric

FOLD

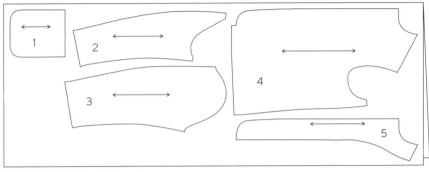

SELVEDGE

150 cm (60 in.) wide fabric

Interfacing

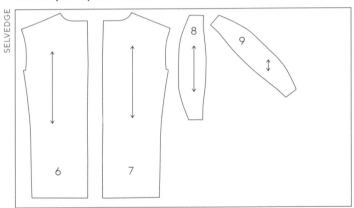

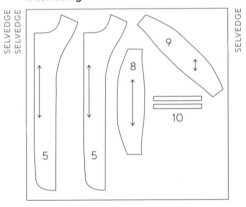

1   Pocket – cut 2

2   Under sleeve – cut 2

3   Top sleeve – cut 2

4   Front jacket – cut 2

5   Facing – cut 2 in main and 2 in interfacing

6   Left back – cut 1

7   Right back – cut 1

8   Top collar – cut 1 in main and 1 in interfacing

9   Under collar – cut 1 in main and 1 in interfacing

10 Pocket facing – cut 2 in interfacing

THE SEWING STARTS HERE

1 **Prepare the pieces**
Following the manufacturer's instructions, apply interfacing to the top collar and under collar, the front facings and the top edges of the pockets.

2 **Construct the back**
With wrong sides together, matching the shoulders and neckline, pin the back jacket pieces together along the centre back. One side has a regular 1.5-cm (⅝-in.) seam allowance and the other a seam 2-cm (¾-in.) to enable you to create a felled seam. Stitch the seam, then press the seam allowances to the right-hand side. Trim the smaller seam allowance to 1 cm (⅜ in.). For the seam allowance that's now lying on top, press under the raw edge by 1 cm (⅜ in.). Fold this edge over to enclose the trimmed seam allowance, and topstitch on the edge.

3 **Construct the pockets**
Along the top edge of the pockets, press 1.5 cm (⅝ in.) to the wrong side, then press under the interfaced 2 cm (¾ in.) to create a strong top edge. Topstitch in place.

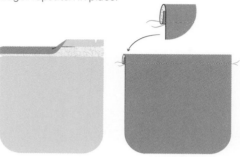

4 Press 1.5 cm (⅝ in.) to the wrong side of the pocket all around the curved edges. Fold the top corners of the seam allowance in diagonally, so they won't peep out of the pocket.

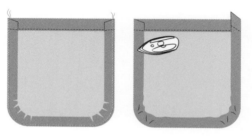

TOP TIP

Stitch a line around the pocket just inside the seam allowance to encourage the pocket seam allowance to fold in: fabric naturally wants to fold around a stitched line. You may need to clip into the seam allowance a little bit, too.

5 Place the pockets on the right side of the front jackets, as indicated on the pattern. Pin in place, using plenty of pins to control the curves. Lower your stitch length to about 2.5 to create a smooth stitch line, and topstitch all around the U-shape.

6 **Construct the front**
With right sides together, pin and sew the fronts of the jacket to the back along the shoulder seams. Overlock the seam allowances together at a foot's width and press towards the back. Topstitch the shoulder seams 5 mm (¼ in.) away from the seams, towards the back.

7 With right sides together, pin and sew the side seams. Overlock the seam allowances together at a foot's width and press towards the back. Topstitch the side seam 5 mm (¼ in.) away from the seam, towards the back.

....

TOP TIP

Check the fit of the main garment at this point and see whether you are happy with the length, the waist and the shoulder length. You could shape the side seam to be a bit more form fitting if you wish.

....

8 Overlock the shoulder and curved edge of both front facings.

9 On the outside of your jacket, in between the lapel notches, lay the raw edge of the under collar against the raw edge of the neckline, right sides together. Pin and sew, then press the collar and all seam allowances upwards.

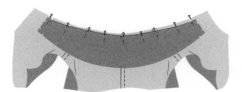

10 With right sides together, matching the shoulder notch on the top collar to the shoulder line on the front facings, pin and sew the top collar to the front facings. Press the seam open and press the seam allowance of the remaining part of the curved collar neckline to the wrong side.

11 Lay the joined facing and top collar right sides together on top of the jacket. Pin and sew the top collar to the under collar along the outside edge. Press the seam open and understitch along the under collar.

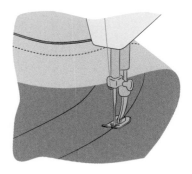

12 Lay the joined facing and top collar back on top of the outside of the jacket and pin the front facing to the front edge of the jacket. Sew up to the lapel corner. Trim the seam allowances to 1 cm (⅜ in.).

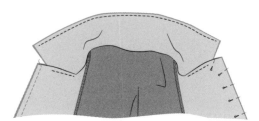

13 Sew the remaining L-shape of the collar and the top of the facing. Trim the seam allowances to 5 mm (¼ in.) and trim the corners away.

14 Turn the facing and collar right side out to the inside of the jacket and press well. Slipstitch the collar to the seam allowance around the back neckline. Hand sew the facing shoulder to the inside shoulder seam.

15 On the outside of the jacket, topstitch 5 mm (¼ in.) away from the edge all around the front facing's centre front edge, lapel and top edge of the collar.

16 **Construct the two-piece sleeves**
With right sides together, pin and sew the top
sleeve to the under sleeve along the back seam.
Overlock the seam allowances together at a
foot's width and press towards the under sleeve.
From the right side of the sleeve, topstitch 5 mm
(¼ in.) from the seam towards the back. With right
sides together again, pin and sew the remaining
sleeve seam. Overlock the seam allowances
together at a foot's width and press the seam
towards the back. Turn the sleeve right side out.
Repeat for the second sleeve.

17 Hem the sleeves: the hem allowance is 3 cm
(1¼ in.), so you could turn up 1 cm and then
2 cm (⅜ in. and then ¾ in.) to create this, or
1.5 cm and 1.5 cm (⅝ in. and ⅝ in.). Stitch
close to the folded edge.

18 With right sides together, pin the sleeves into the
armholes, making sure you match the notches.
Sew in place, starting from the underarm. The
shoulder point should match the shoulder seam.
There will be some ease around the sleeve head,
which you will see as excess material once you
have matched the notches and have started
pinning from the underarm up.

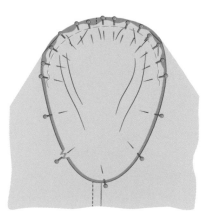

TOP TIP

If you struggle to distribute the ease with pins only,
run a gathering stitch within the seam allowance of
the sleeve head and use that to draw up the sleeve
head to fit the armhole. The ease should be centred
around the shoulder point, with a little bit more
towards the back for shoulder movement.

19 Prepare bias binding for the armhole seam allowances, making one side slightly wider than the other (see Special Feature, page 71). Trim the armhole seam allowance so that it's narrow enough for you to be able to slot the binding over it. Pin the binding all the way around the armhole. Starting at the underarm, sew all the way around, neatly encasing all the seam allowances. Stop 2 cm (¾ in.) from the end, trim the binding if necessary and fold the raw short edge of the binding under for a neat finish. Finish your stitch at the underarm.

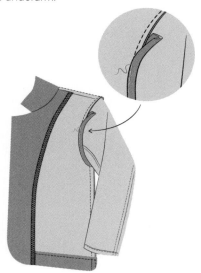

20 Finish the jacket
Hem the jacket with a double-turned hem, stitching close to the folded edge. As on the sleeves, the total hem allowance is 3 cm (1¼ in.); see step 17.

21 Secure the facing from the inside of the garment by stitching within the overlocking along the edge of the facing, attaching the facing to the jacket. This stitch line will be visible on the right side of the jacket. Hand stitch the shoulder of the facing to the inside shoulder seam.

22 Make horizontal buttonholes on the left front of the jacket (as worn), positioning the first one at the break point (where the centre front edge turns into the lapel, indicated on your pattern), and spacing the rest evenly down the front, with the last one roughly 15 cm (6 in.) from the bottom. Attach buttons to the right front to correspond.

SPECIAL TECHNIQUE: BUTTONS AND BUTTONHOLES

Button stands

The button stand is the area of the garment that holds the buttons on one side and the buttonholes on the other side. Button stands can either be 'grown on' (part of the front garment pattern, as in the Jumpsuit on page 161) or attached separately (as in the Pussybow Blouse on page 51). The button stand is the same size left and right, and the way you overlap them depends on whether the garment is for a man or a woman. Men's garments overlap wearer's left over right; women's garments overlap wearer's right over left.

Horizontal or vertical buttonholes?

Vertical buttonholes allow for a more accurate fit, as the buttons can't move from side to side once buttoned up. They are suitable for shirt fronts, dresses and skirts. Horizontal buttonholes allow the button to slide around, which allows for a bit more movement. For this reason, the top buttonhole on a shirt, cuff, coat or jacket is horizontal.

What size buttonholes?

The buttonhole for an average button should be 3 mm (⅛ in.) longer than the button. If you are using very thick buttons, you will need to make the buttonhole slightly bigger. Many new sewing machines come with a buttonhole presser foot where you can measure the size of your button to get the exact size buttonhole.

TOP TIPS

- A buttonhole cutter, which looks like a mini chisel, will make opening your buttonholes a breeze!
- Always have an odd number of buttons, as this works better for positioning.
- Buttons never go all the way down on a garment. Look at jackets and button-down shirts in your wardrobe and see where the last button is positioned.

Where to position your buttonholes

The centre front of your buttoned-up garment will lie somewhere along the middle of the button stand. This should be indicated on your pattern. When you overlap your button stands, the centre front lines will lie on top of each other. The buttons and buttonholes will be positioned along this line.

- Buttons go right on top of the centre front line.
- Horizontal buttonholes should start 3 mm (⅛ in.) from the centre line towards the edge of the garment.
- Vertical buttonholes go right on top of the centre front line.

For women's garments, always have a button at the two stress points of the button stand – the fullest part of the bust and the waist. Position these two buttons first, plus the very top button, and then space the other buttons evenly along the button stand.

For a jacket or a coat with a lapel, such as the Linen Jacket, the point where the lapel changes into the centre front of the garment is called the 'break point'. Position the top button here. The position of the break point may be indicated on the pattern, but it's a good idea to fit this on the wearer to make sure it's suited to the person's body shape.

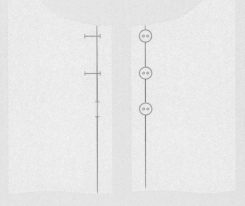

RECYCLE & RE-USE CLOTHING

The average person in Britain owns 167 items of clothing in their wardrobe. This adds up to a lot of shirts, dresses, trousers, jumpers, playsuits and shorts. During the past decade, clothing and textiles have become the fastest-growing stream of waste in the United Kingdom and now represent the fifth biggest environmental footprint of any industry. Read on to find out how to recycle and re-use your clothing, giving your much loved (or even unloved) items a new lease of life.

FABRIC AND CLOTHING SWAPS

Fabric swaps are becoming ever more popular within the sewing community, which is fantastic! More and more of you are organising mini swaps with your friends as well as large-scale fabric swaps at sewing meet-ups and events. Fabric swaps are a fantastic way of combatting textile waste. We all have a fabric in our collection that we can no longer envision using and that's okay: styles can change. Your unwanted bolt of polka-dot cotton fabric could be someone else's dream! If you would like to organise your own fabric swap, you can create an event on social media or email your favourite sewing bloggers to spread the word. You can also put on a clothing swap, which is another fantastic way to reduce fabric and clothing waste.

TOP TIP

Make a tag for any fabrics you want to swap describing what the fabric composition is (for example, 100% viscose), as well as the length and width of the piece. This makes fabric swaps much more efficient, making sure no unwanted fabrics are left behind after the event.

RE-USE WHAT YOU ALREADY OWN

This might be an obvious one but some of us can often forget what we already own. The most sustainable item of clothing is one that's already hanging in your wardrobe. Before starting a new sewing project or fabric shop, check what your already own. It might surprise you!

UPCYCLE AND REPURPOSE

This is a creative and fun thing to do when it comes to clothing that has seen better days or items in your wardrobe you find you no longer wear. You can turn a man's shirt into a blouse, bed sheets into a dress, jeans into a pinafore, a jumpsuit into trousers. The possibilities are endless! You can even take apart a previous garment and use the fabric to make something completely new.

Look at the original features of the garment you wish to upcycle – collars, frills, pockets and button plackets – and use them as a base to create a new garment. See page 142 for upcycling inspiration, complete with a tutorial on how to make your own pinafore skirt from unwanted jeans.

EMBROIDERY

Embroidery has been around since 30,000 BC and it has made an amazing resurgence in the craft community as well as the fashion industry. In the last few years catwalks and the highstreet have been adorned with embroidery. It is a creative way of giving an old item of clothing a fresh new look. It can be used to fix clothes that have been damaged or stained, as well as to embellish.

RECYCLE

Many high-street stores now take your unwanted clothes to be recycled. This process can't always be traced, so also check your local rubbish collection provider to see if they recycle textiles.

TOP TIP

When recycling, remove any buttons or zips. You can re-use them in future sewing projects or give them to a friend who has just started sewing.

DONATE

If you no longer love a garment in your wardrobe, whether it's homemade or shop bought, you can swap or donate it. Only donate clothing that is in a sellable condition, because that way you know there is a very low chance of it ending up in landfill, if it doesn't sell. You can donate clothing to charity shops or women's shelters, as these are among many other organisations that are in need of clothing. You can even donate your unwanted fabrics to schools and colleges that run art and fashion courses. This is incredibly valuable to the students and your donation will be used for educational purposes.

Women's Blouse

Turn a form-fitting man's or (woman's) shirt into a floaty blouse, re-using the top part of the shirt and creating an empire seam under the bust with the fabric that originally formed the body of the shirt.

You can reuse the parts of the shirt in your new blouse or add a different fabric, depending on what you have decided to make and how much material you need. If you decide to add another material, choose a fabric of a similar weight to the shirt for the best effect.

Materials

- Man's shirt
- Basic sewing kit (see page 14)

1 Decide how long you want the sleeves to be; we opted for a ¾-length sleeve for the version shown here. Cut the sleeves about 1.5 cm (⅝ in.) longer than the desired finished length, so that you have some material for the seam allowance. Then cut the cuffs off about 1.5 cm (⅝ in.) above the cuff. Sew the cuffs back on in the new position. You will have to gather the sleeves to achieve this. When you've sewn the cuffs in place, overlock the seam. We also cut the collar off to make a wide, rounded neckline.

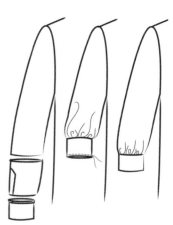

2 Cut across the shirt all the way around, either under the bust (for the empire seam shown here) or at waist level, so that it is now in two halves. Cut 1.5 cm (⅝ in.) below the desired seam line so that you have a seam allowance. Gather the cut edges of both halves, then sew them back together again, taking care to align the button bands of the two halves. Overlock the seam allowance.

3 Adjust the length if needed by hemming the new blouse with a narrow double hem.

Variation

Instead of gathering the top half, you could insert bust darts to create more shape. You can insert a bust dart under the fullest part of each breast by pinning this when you are trying it on.

NATURAL DYES

Freshen up an old garment with natural dye for a new look. We dyed our blouse on page 188 with avocado stones to get this beautiful pink colour! Here is the recipe for you to try at home, using only two natural ingredients. You will need up to six stones for a project like this, but the more you have the stronger the colour will be. Avocado pits contain a natural tannin, which helps bind the colour onto cotton and linen fibres.

Materials needed

- 1 litre (2 pints) soya milk
- 6 avocado stones (you can also use the skins if you wish)
- Container with a lid
- Dye pot (use an aluminium pot for best results, or a stainless steel pan; make sure it's big enough for your item!)
- Gloves
- Wooden spoon to stir

PRE-SOAK THE FABRIC

1   Pre-wash your shirt/fabric either by hand or in a washing machine without detergent.

2   Pour 1 litre (2 pints) of soya milk into a container with a lid and top up with cold water until you have enough liquid to cover your fabric. The soya milk acts as a mordant, helping to prepare the fabric in advance to bind with the dye.

3   Add the shirt/fabric to the container. Stir every so often to ensure for an even coverage, then cover the container and leave in a cool place for 12 hours.

4   After the first soak, squeeze the excess liquid out and spin in a washing machine on the spin cycle; don't empty the container. Hang to dry.

5   When the fabric is fully dry, return it to the soya milk for another 3–5 hours, then spin and dry as before. Repeat the process again, so that the fabric has been soaked in the soya milk three times. If the soya milk starts to split or ferment, then replace it with new milk. The more you pre-soak your fabric, the more colour it will absorb in the dyeing process.

PREPARE THE DYE POT

1   Cut the avocado stones into quarters or halves and place them in your dye pot. You can also use the avocado skins – just make sure they're dried properly. (You can do this by gently cleaning them out to ensure no flesh is left and then dry them out in an oven on a low heat or on top of a radiator.) You can store your avocados and skins in the freezer before you are ready to use them. Keep them in a sealed container to prevent them from going mouldy.

2   Fill your dye pot with 1–2 litres (2–4 pints) of water and bring to the boil. Turn the heat down low and simmer for 1 hour to extract the natural tannin and colour from the pits and skins.

3 After 1 hour, take the pan off the heat and leave the avocado dye stand for 24 hours.

4 Drain the dye liquid through a sieve and muslin to gather any bits from the avocados. Pour the liquid back into your dye pot.

DYEING PROCESS

1 Once your fabric has had its last soak and is fully dry, wet it thoroughly in cold water to ensure you obtain an even dye. Place in the dye pot. You may need to add extra water to cover the fabric.

2 Bring the dye to a gentle boil and simmer for 40–60 minutes. Take the pot off heat and let it stand for 2 hours, stirring often. You can leave your shirt in the dye for a further 24 hours to obtain a stronger colour.

3 Rinse in cold water and then place in a washing machine for a short spin and hang to dry.

TOP TIP

Aftercare: wash your shirt in a pH-balanced detergent, as this can affect the colour after dyeing.

Halterneck Dress

This feminine dress is perfect for a touch of Hollywood-style glamour. Wear it to a party with a bright lipstick or on holiday with wedges and a straw bag. The fitted halter neck and fully lined bodice gives it a classic vintage look. This pattern is suitable for improving makers, as the darts and neckline will require precision. For experienced makers, this is a great dress to test your skills in taking the darts in or letting them out to achieve the perfect fit (see page 33).

TO MAKE THE HALTERNECK DRESS

Materials

- Sizes 4–10: 2 m (2¼ yd) fabric 150 cm (60 in.) wide
- Sizes 12–18: 2.3 m (3½ yd) fabric 150 cm (60 in.) wide
- 70 cm (¾ yd) lining fabric (this can be the same as your top fabric)
- 30 cm (12 in.) interfacing
- 21-cm (8-in.) invisible zip
- 2 flat skirt hooks and bars
- Small hook and eye for the top of the zip (optional)
- Basic sewing kit (see page 14)

Difficulty level

Improvers

Fabric suggestions

Choose a fabric with plenty of drape, such as rayon, bamboo silk, viscose or silk.

Design notes

Use a 1.5-cm (⅝-in.) seam allowance throughout, unless otherwise stated.

Instructions are given for overlocking the seam allowances, but if you don't have an overlocker you can neaten the seam allowances by zigzagging them instead.

Finished measurements	4	6	8	10	12	14	16	18
Front skirt length (cm)	71.5	71.5	71.5	71.5	71.5	71.5	71.5	71.5
Front skirt length (in.)	28⅛	28⅛	28⅛	28⅛	28⅛	28⅛	28⅛	28⅛
Back skirt length (cm)	64	64	64	64	64	64	64	64
Back skirt length (in.)	25¼	25¼	25¼	25¼	25¼	25¼	25¼	25¼
Waist (cm)	67	72	77	82	87	92	97	102
Waist (in.)	26⅜	28⅜	30⅜	32¼	34¼	36¼	38⅛	40⅛
Hem width (cm)	434.5	439.5	444.5	449.4	454.5	459.5	464.5	469.5
Hem width (in.)	171	173	175	177	179	181	183	185

CUTTING GUIDE

150 cm (60 in.) wide fabric

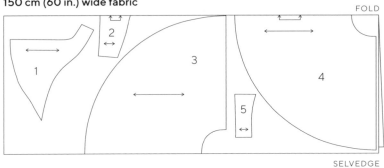

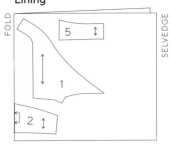

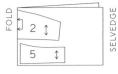

FOLD

SELVEDGE

1 Front bodice – cut 2 in main and lining

2 Front waistband – cut 1 on the fold in main, lining and interfacing

3 Skirt back – cut 2

4 Skirt front – cut 1 on fold

5 Back waistband – cut 2 in main, lining and interfacing

Lining

FOLD

SELVEDGE

Interfacing

FOLD

SELVEDGE

THE SEWING STARTS HERE

1 Prepare the pieces
Following the manufacturer's instructions, apply interfacing to the wrong side of the main fabric front and back waistbands. Transfer the dart markings to the front bodice lining pieces and the pleat indications to the front bodice pieces.

2 Construct the front bodice
Staystitch the front neck edge of each front bodice and each front bodice lining 1 cm (⅜ in.) from the edge.

3 Pin the darts on the front bodice lining pieces and sew from the side edge to the point. Don't backstitch at the point of the dart: run off exactly where the dart finishes, leave a tail of thread and tie it off by hand. This way you get a perfect point. Press the darts towards the side seams.

4 Following the pattern, fold the eight pleats in each front bodice (see Special Technique, page 124). Machine tack within the seam allowance to hold them in place.

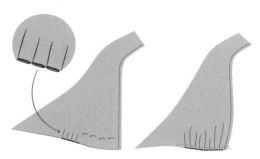

5 Place one front bodice and the corresponding front bodice lining right sides together. Pin and sew along the centre front neck edge. Clip around the curved edges and press the seam open. Press the seam allowances towards the lining. Repeat with the remaining bodice and lining pieces.

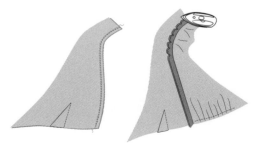

6 From the right side, understitch the seam allowance to the bodice lining, stopping 2 cm (¾ in.) from the back neck edge.

7 Fold back the bodice and bodice lining to that they're right sides together again. Pin the outer edges together and sew. Trim the seam allowance to 5 mm (¼ in.) and gently press the seam open.

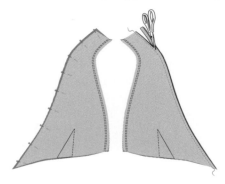

8 Pin along the short edge of the back neck seam and sew. Trim the seam allowance to 5 mm (¼ in.) and trim the corners.

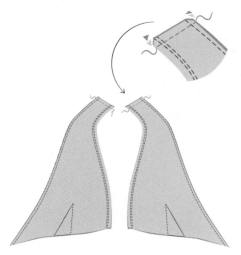

9 Turn both bodice pieces right side out. Press and roll the seams slightly towards the lining, using plenty of steam – but be careful not to stretch the bodice out of shape by pulling along the curves. Use a bamboo pointer on the corners of the neck for a crisp finish.

10 Pin the two layers of each bodice section together along the bottom edge. Sew 5 mm (¼ in.) from the raw edge to hold the layers in place. Gently ease the lining layer until it matches the raw edge of the outer bodice layer. Press the seam gently at the edge, being careful not to press the pleats too much.

11 **Construct the waistband**
With right sides together, matching the seams, pin the interfaced front and back waistband pieces together. Stitch and press the seams open. Repeat with the waistband lining pieces.

12 Pin the front bodice pieces along the top of the main fabric (interfaced) waistband, right sides together and matching the notches at the centre front and side seams. Pin and stitch in place.

13 Place the (non-interfaced) waistband lining on top, right side down, so that the front bodice is sandwiched in between the two waistband pieces. Pin all the layers together and stitch them together on the same stitch line, starting and stopping approximately 4 cm (1½ in.) from the centre back edges of the waistband. Turn the bodice right side out and press the waistband and lining seam allowances downwards. Along the unsewn edge of the waistband lining, press 1.5 cm (⅝ in.) to the wrong side.

14 **Construct the skirt**
Staystitch around the waist of the skirt pieces 1 cm (⅜ in.) from the raw edges, stitching within the seam allowance.

15 With right sides together, matching the zip notches, pin the centre back seam of the skirt. Sew in place from the zip notch down, backstitching at the bottom of the zip notch, leaving the top of the seam open. Press the seam open and overlock both sides of the seam allowance separately.

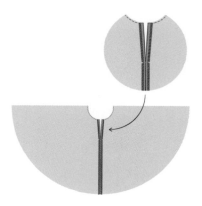

16 Pin the front and back skirts right sides together, matching the side seams. Stitch and press the seams open, then overlock both sides of the seam allowance separately.

17 Attach the bodice to the skirt
Place the raw bottom edge of the main fabric waistband against the raw edge of the skirt waist, right sides together. The bodice will be lying upside down. Pin the waistband in place all the way around the waistline edge, matching the side seams of the bodice with the side seams of the skirt, and matching the notches. Stitch all the way around. Press the seam allowances up towards the bodice.

18 Pin the invisible zip into the centre back opening of the skirt, making sure that the back waistband lining is out the way. Stitch in place (see page 28).

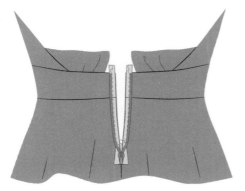

19 Fold the lining pieces of the back waistband over to the right side of the dress waistband, so that the lining and main fabric waistbands are right sides together. Pin in place along the short centre back edge.

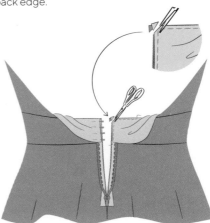

20 Stitch along the back upper edge and down the centre back edge, sandwiching the zip in between the layers. Trim the centre back corner edges and then fold through to the correct side of the fabric and press the seam.

21 On the inside of your dress, pin the pressed-under edge of the lining waistband to the seam allowance of the waistband seam, matching up the centre front, the side seams and the centre back seams. Stitch the lining in place by hand or stitch in the ditch from the outside (see page 81, step 12).

22 Finish the dress
At the back neck of your dress, sew two flat skirt hooks underneath the right neck and two flat bars to the upper side of the left neck opening.

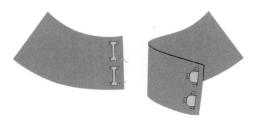

23 Before hemming your dress, hang it up for a few days to allow the fabric to drop. If you have made your dress in a silky, fine fabric, hem your skirt with a rolled hem on the overlocker; consult your overlocker manual. If you have made your dress in a more stable fabric, overlock the entire hem and then turn up by 5 mm (¼ in.), carefully pinning the hem all around to distribute the fullness.

TOP TIPS

° You can check whether the hem has dropped by hanging the dress on a mannequin and measuring the distance between the hem and the floor; it should be the same all the way around. If it has dropped in places, you can level it to be the same as the rest of the hem.

° Be careful not to stretch the hem as you go around, unless you want a fluted hem.

° Because this a full circle skirt, you can't do a very big hem: the circumference of the hem will be greater at the raw edge than the point you're stitching it to, so the smaller the hem the better.

Tablecloth Dress

Have you ever inherited a pretty tablecloth, or bought one from a vintage shop but never used it? Why not make it into something beautiful that you can wear on a daily basis? A blouse or dress like this is very easy to make and you can choose the prettiest part of the linen to use around the neckline.

Materials

- Vintage tablecloth for the yoke (one with colourful embroidery or pretty whitework)
- Fabric for the lower half of the garment
- Bias binding for the neck opening (optional)
- Basic sewing kit (see page 14)

1 First, determine the size of the yoke of your garment. For a sleeveless garment, measure from shoulder to shoulder for the width, and from the hollow of your front neck to under your bust, multiplied by 2, for the length. If you want sleeves, have someone measure you from mid arm to mid arm, with your arms outstretched, and use that as the width. Add 3-cm (1¼-in.) hem and seam allowances. Cut a rectangle to the required size from the vintage tablecloth.

2 Find the centre of the rectangle by folding it in half both horizontally and vertically and marking it. Use a patternmaster to draw a neck opening in the middle, so that 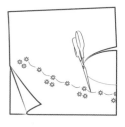 you can put the garment on over your head. If you don't have a pattern-making tool like this, fold the fabric in half and draw half an oval, so that when you cut it out it's symmetrical on both sides. A neckline is always lower towards the front of the body and higher around the back neck.

3 For the body of the blouse or dress, cut two rectangles from leftover linen or a new fabric. To work out the width, add roughly 50 cm (20 in.) to the rectangle that you drew previously. To work out the length, decide if you want to make a blouse or dress and measure from your underbust to the desired length; remember to add 3 cm (1¼ in.) for the hem. We used a vintage sheet and left the original hem on it; we simply cut it in half to make up the front and back and gathered the whole width.

4 With the pieces lying flat in front of you, gather the top edges of the two big rectangles to fit the yoke front and back. Pin the large rectangles and yoke right sides together, and sew. Overlock the seams.

5 Fold the garment in half with right sides together and sew the underarm and side seams in one go. If you are making a sleeveless garment, you can hem the armhole of the yoke first and then simply sew down the sides of the rectangles. Overlock the seams.

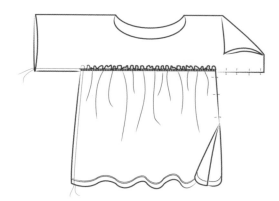

6 Finish the neckline. We finished our neckline with a narrow rolled hem, but bias binding is a very neat alternative method.

7 Hem the sleeves and the garment.

Bomber Jacket

A classic that has stood the test of time, this jacket is a wardrobe staple for wearers of all ages. It's the type of jacket that bridges seasons and crosses the line between indoor and outdoor wear. You can make it as fun or as classic as you like through your choice of fabric: choose a bold floral or a geometric print for a fashion statement or a solid colour for a more verstaile look. We used a polyester shell, which is an ideal fabric for a classic bomber jacket, but you can mix it up by using fabric scraps for different elements of the jacket.

TO MAKE THE BOMBER JACKET

Materials

- 2 m (2¼ yd) fabric 150 cm (60 in.) wide
- 50 cm (20 in.) stretch ribbing for cuffs and waistband
- 70 cm (¾ yd) interfacing
- 61-cm (24-in.) open-ended zip
- Basic sewing kit (see page 14)

Difficulty level

Advanced

Fabric suggestions

Shell fabrics made from polyester, medium denim, heavy linen and faux leather are suitable. For the cuffs and waistband, you can choose matching ribbing or go all out with a contrasting colour.

Design notes

Use a 1.5-cm (⅝-in.) seam allowance throughout, unless otherwise stated.

Instructions are given for overlocking the seam allowances, but if you don't have an overlocker you can neaten the seam allowances by zigzagging them instead.

Finished measurements	34	36	38	40	42	44
Front length (cm)	68	68.5	69	69.5	70	70.5
Front length (in.)	26¾	27	27⅛	27⅜	27½	27¾
Back length (cm)	73	73.5	74	74.5	75	75.5
Back length (in.)	28¾	29	29⅛	29⅜	29½	29¾
Chest (cm)	115	120	125	130	135	140
Chest (in.)	45¼	47¼	49¼	51¼	53¼	55⅛
Waist (cm)	115	120	125	130	135	140
Waist (in.)	45¼	47¼	49¼	51⅕	53¼	55⅛
Sleeve length (cm)	55	55.5	56	56.5	57	57.5
Sleeve length (in.)	21½	21¾	22	22¼	22½	22¾
Shoulder (cm)	18	18	18.5	18.5	19	19.5
Shoulder (in.)	7	7	7¼	7¼	7½	7⅜

CUTTING GUIDE

150 cm (60 in.) wide fabric

FOLD

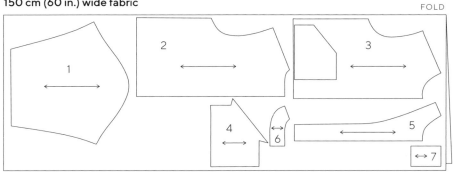

SELVEDGE

Ribbing FOLD   **Interfacing** FOLD

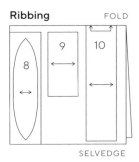

SELVEDGE

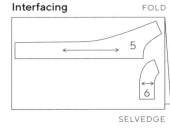

SELVEDGE

1   Sleeve – cut 2
2   Back jacket – cut 2
3   Front jacket – cut 2
4   Pocket – cut 2
5   Front facing – cut 2 in main and 2 in interfacing
6   Back neck facing – cut 2 in main and 2 in interfacing

7   Zip tab – cut 2
8   Collar – cut 1 in ribbing
9   Sleeve cuff – cut 2 in ribbing
10   Waistband – cut 1 on the fold in ribbing

Cropped Bomber Jacket (page 216)

150 cm (60 in.) wide fabric

FOLD   **Interfacing** FOLD   **Ribbing** FOLD

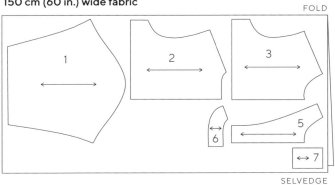

SELVEDGE

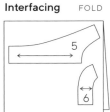

SELVEDGE

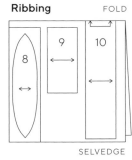

SELVEDGE

THE SEWING STARTS HERE

1 Prepare the pieces
Following the manufacturer's instructions, apply interfacing to the wrong side of the front facings and back neck facings. Overlock the outer edge of the back neck and front facings.

2 Construct the pockets
Press the pocket opening to the wrong side by 1 cm (⅜ in.) and then by 1.5 cm (⅝ in.) and pin in place. Sew in place 1 cm (⅜ in.) from the pocket edge. Repeat on the second pocket.

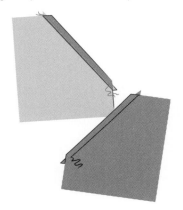

3 Overlock the top edge and both side edges of the pockets. Press these edges under by 1.5 cm (⅝ in.), using plenty of steam. Leave the bottom of the pockets as a raw unfolded edge.

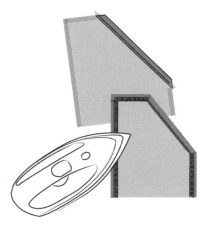

TOP TIP

Press the folds in place and leave to cool; this will make it easier to pin the pockets onto the jacket in the next step

4 Pin the pockets to the jacket fronts, referring to the pattern for the placement. Stitch two rows of topstitching across the top and sides. Remember not to sew the pocket opening to the jacket! Across the bottom edge of the pocket, sew a row of machine tacking within the seam allowance to hold the pocket in place.

5 Insert the zip
With right sides together, aligning the edge of the tab with the centre front edge, pin the zip tab to the bottom of the jacket. Starting from the centre front edge, sew the tab in, stopping 1.5 cm (⅝ in.) short of the other edge of the tab; this will be attached to the ribbing in step 24. Press the seam allowance open. Repeat with the other tab and jacket front.

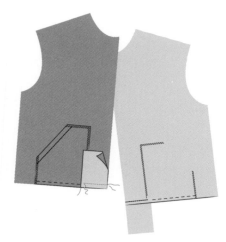

7 Unfold the zip-line crease, so that the whole of the jacket front is right side up. Separate the two halves of your open-ended zip. Place the zip face down, with the teeth along the zip-line crease, matching the bottom of the zip with the fold line on the zip tab. The top of the zip should reach the top of the front jacket. Pin in place, then sew 5 mm (¼ in.) from the edge of the zip tape. Attach the other half of the zip to the other jacket front.

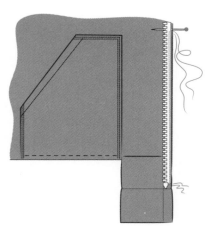

6 Fold the zip tab down. Fold the centre front and tab to the wrong side of the jacket along the zip line. Press in place. Repeat on the second jacket front.

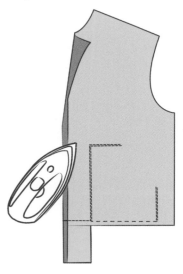

8 With right sides together, pin the bottom edge of the front facing to the bottom of the zip tab, centring it on the zip tab so that there is a 1-cm (⅜-in.) gap on each side. Sew in place across the bottom edge and press the seam open. Repeat with the remaining front and front facing.

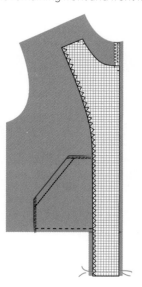

9 Keeping the facing and jacket right sides together, bring the facing up to meet the neckline. This will effectively fold the zip tab in half along the fold line. Pin the facing in place along the centre front. Start sewing from the fold line of the zip tab upwards, sandwiching the zip in the middle, and stop 2 cm (¾ in.) from the top of the front at the neckline. Repeat with the remaining front and front facing.

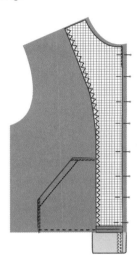

10 Turn the facing to the wrong side of the jacket front so that the facing and jacket are wrong sides together. Press towards the inside of the jacket.

11 **Construct the back and shoulders**
With right sides together, pin and sew the back pieces together along the centre back. Overlock both seam allowances together and press the seam to the left. Working on the right side of the jacket, topstitch the seam 5 mm (¼ in.) from the edge (towards the right back).

12 With right sides together, pin the fronts to the back at the shoulder seams, and sew; don't include the facing in this shoulder seam. Overlock the seam allowances together and press towards the back of the jacket.

13 Lay the jacket out flat, right side up. With right sides together, matching the notches on the sleeve head to the jacket armhole, pin the sleeves to the jacket. Sew in place and overlock the seam allowances together at a foot's width. Press towards the body of the jacket. Topstitch 5 mm (¼ in.) from the seam on the body of the jacket.

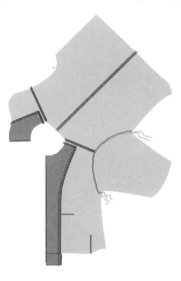

14 Fold the garment right sides together, matching the underarm and side edges. Pin and sew the side seam and underarm seams on each side. Overlock the seam allowances together and press towards the back of the jacket.

15 Construct the collar and facing
Fold the ribbed collar in half along the fold line, wrong sides together, and press. Matching the notches at the centre back, shoulder seams and centre front, pin the collar in place on the right side of the jacket so that the curved neck edge of the collar matches the jacket neckline. You will need to stretch the ribbing slightly around the neckline for it to fit. Stitch the collar seam all the way around. Press the seam allowance down towards the hem of the jacket.

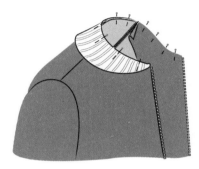

16 Pin and sew the back neck facings right sides together along the centre back. Press the seam open and overlock the raw edges.

17 With right sides together, pin the shoulders of the back facing to the shoulders of the front facings. To do this, it's easiest to have the front facings folded to the outside of the garment again. Sew and press the seams open. Pin the facing in place around the neckline of the jacket, sandwiching the collar piece in between.

18 Sew the facing, ribbed collar and jacket layers together around the neckline, continuing 2 cm (¾ in.) down the centre front to join the previous stitch line. Trim the corners of the front facing at the centre front. Fold the facing to the inside of the jacket. Press and roll the seam edge slightly to the inside, using a bamboo pointer to push out the corners for a neat finish.

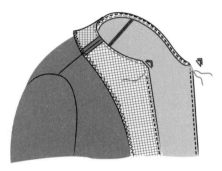

19 Turn the jacket right side out and topstitch 5 mm (¼ in.) from the edge, stitching from the bottom of the zip tab along the zip line, up to the front neck, around the back neck and back down to the bottom of the zip tab. Gently press the topstitching.

20 Construct the cuffs
Fold the cuffs in half lengthways, right sides together, matching the short sides and notches. Pin and sew. Press the seams open. Fold the cuffs in half widthways, wrong sides together, and press. Pin around the raw edges and machine tack together within the seam allowance.

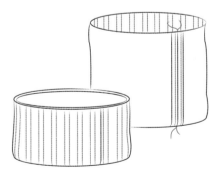

21 Place the cuffs over the sleeves, aligning the raw edges. Pin in place, matching the cuff side seams to the sleeve underarm seams. Sew in place: you will need to stretch the ribbed cuff slightly to fit the sleeve. Press the seams up towards the shoulders and overlock the seam allowances together at a foot's width.

22 Turn the cuffs down so that the seams are on the inside of the sleeve. Topstitch the cuffs' overlocked seam to the jacket sleeves 5 mm (¼ in.) from the seam.

23 Construct the waistband
Fold the ribbed waistband piece in half lengthways, right sides together, and press.

24 Slide the folded waistband over the zip tab to encase the zip tab. You should see the wrong side of the waistband. Pin and sew through all the layers, stopping where the zip tab meets the facing. Repeat on the other side of the jacket, taking care not to twist the waistband.

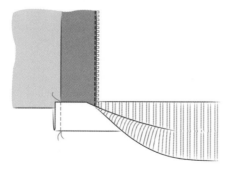

25 Turn the waistband to the right side. It should now be attached along the zip tabs only – the waist of the jacket and the waistband are still unattached.

26 Fold the waistband to the right side of the jacket, so the right sides are together. Pin the raw edge of the waistband to the bottom edge of the jacket, matching the notches at the centre back and side seams. (The waistband will need to stretch to fit the jacket hem.) Start and finish stitching from the point where the facing attaches to the zip tab. Stitch the seam, overlock the seam allowances together at a foot's width, then press the seam up towards the shoulder. Give the seam a good press to help the ribbing shrink back into place after stretching. Fold the finished waistband down.

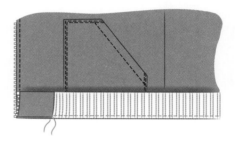

27 On the right side of the jacket, topstitch 5 mm (¼ in.) from the end of the zip along the zip tab, along the edge of the jacket and above the waistband.

Cropped Bomber Jacket

This pattern hack gives you the option of making the classic men's bomber jacket into a shorter, more playful-looking garment, without pockets. The fit on this garment is unisex, as the only change is the length. If you have machine embroidery skills, why not embroider a motif on the back?

For details of how many of each piece to cut, refer to the cutting guide on page 207.

Difficulty level

Advanced

Materials

- 1.5 m (1¾ yd) fabric 150 cm (60 in.) wide
- 50 cm (20 in.) stretch ribbing for cuffs and waistband
- 45 c m (17¾ in.) interfacing
- 31-cm (12-in.) open ended metal zip
- Basic sewing kit (see page 14)

1 Cut out the pieces, using the shorter cutting line on the back, front and front facing pattern pieces and omitting the pockets.

2 Omitting steps 1–4, make up the jacket following the instructions for the Bomber Jacket on pages 210–214.

Finished measurements	34	36	38	40	42	44
Front length cropped (cm)	43	43.5	44	44.5	45.5	46
Front length cropped (in.)	17	17⅛	17⅜	17¾	18	18⅛
Back length cropped (cm)	48	48.5	49	50	50.5	51
Back length cropped (in.)	18⅞	19	19¼	19½	19⅞	20
Chest (cm)	115	120	125	130	135	140
Chest (in.)	45¼	47¼	49¼	51¼	53¼	55⅛
Waist (cm)	115	120	125	130	135	140
Waist (in.)	45¼	47¼	49¼	51¼	53¼	55⅛
Sleeve length (cm)	55	55.5	56	56.5	57	57.5
Sleeve length (in.)	21½	21¾	22	22¼	22½	22¾
Shoulder (cm)	18	18	18.5	18.5	19	19.5
Shoulder (in.)	7	7	7¼	7¼	7½	7⅜

MENDING: DARNING & PATCHING

When your clothes are well loved and well worn, it's inevitable that you will have to fix something at some point. We will assume you know how to reattach a button and fix a hem, as those are easy fixes we are all familiar with. Below you will find some tips on how to mend by darning and patching.

DARNING FOR WOOLLEN GARMENTS

A hole in a woollen garment is fixed by darning and you can use a handy tool called a darning mushroom for this. This is particularly useful for areas like elbows on sweaters, but it will work for most things. Make sure you tie off any broken yarn so that you have a clean working area that won't unravel further. Select your yarns and weave back and forth over the hole with horizontal and vertical lines, until you have remade the missing patch. You can do this invisibly by selecting the same colour yarn or make a feature out of it.

You can use the same technique on fabric, but you should zigzag stitch around the hole first.

1 Trim off any loose yarns around the hole. Work long vertical stitches close together until the hole is covered.

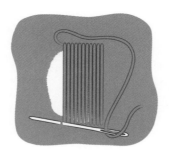

2 Work across the hole, weaving the thread or yarn over and under alternate vertical threads, keeping each row as close as possible to the previous one.

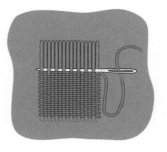

TOP TIP

If you are darning a garment, think about the different colours present in the garment and go for a mix of colours for the threads you use to darn. Do your jeans have white, light blue and darker blue tones in the fibres? Then darn with those three colours and it will blend in much more naturally as you are mimicking the original fabric.

FIXING A STRAIGHT TEAR

This easy fix works well on fine fabrics, as it doesn't add a lot of weight to the repair. If you have a straight tear in a garment, cut yourself a piece of interfacing and position it behind the tear, with the glue side facing the wrong side of the garment. Bring the edges of the tear close together so that they appear seamless. You may have to get rid of any pulled fibres that make it look fuzzy; snip these off with a pair of small, sharp scissors. Then put your iron on top to fuse the interfacing to the back of the garment.

TOP TIP

Prevent glue from getting onto your iron's hotplate by placing a piece of fabric in between the iron and the garment.

PATCHING A HOLE

Use this technique to fix a hole in a garment. The machine stitches ensure that the patch is securely attached so that it lies flush and the edges of the hole can't snag on anything.

1   Snip off any loose threads around the hole so that you have a clean working area.

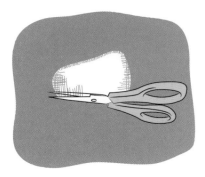

2 Cut out a piece of material as close to the garment's colour as possible and roughly 2 cm (¾ in.) bigger all around. Pin the piece of material behind the hole and then darn over it by hand or use a machine. If you wish, you can tack the patch in place before you start to stop it from moving.

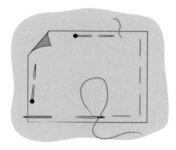

3 Darn over the patch by zigzagging all over it from the right side; make sure you zigzag over the raw edges to fix the patch in place. You can also machine stitch over the patch with a freehand embroidery foot.

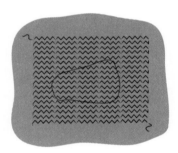

You can do this by hand as well, by working small running stitches across it, either invisibly (see Darning for woollen garments, page 218) or visibly. The visible way of doing this is a Japanese mending technique called sashiko.

Using thread in a contrasting colour, work running stitches, small cross stitches or even star-shaped stitches across the patch to fix it in place.

A SNAGGED FIBRE

If you have a little thread sticking out on the surface of a garment, it can either be a snagged fibre, which is intact, or a broken fibre. In both cases you can thread up a needle and tie the end of the sewing thread to the pulled fibre. You can then pull it back through the surface of the fabric so that it ends up on the back. You can leave a snagged fibre as it is; for a broken fibre, fasten it off at the back to prevent it from unravelling further.

WHY HIDE THE IMPERFECTIONS?

You can have fun with your mending and decide whether you want it to be invisible or to make a feature out of it. There is nothing wrong with imperfections and sometimes highlighting them works better than trying to disguise them. If you have a stain that just won't disappear, why not embroider over it? Or if you have patched a pair of trousers add your own creative flair with some beautiful sashiko-style stitching.

Index

Acknowledgements

LOVE PRODUCTIONS would like to thank the viewers who watch *The Great British Sewing Bee*, especially those who have felt inspired to buy this book. It is the perfect accompaniment to the series thanks to the expertise of authors, Alexandra Bruce and Caroline Akselson, and the dedication of the team at Quadrille, Sarah Lavelle, Harriet Butt, Rebecca Smedley and Katie Jarvis. The clever person behind the design, Emily Lapworth, has helped to produce a covetable book. It is a real privilege to work on *The Great British Sewing Bee* and get to know the sewers behind the gorgeous garments: Alex, Alexei, Ali, Angillia, Ben, Clare, Fiona, Hazel, Janet, Jen, Juliet, Leah, Liz, Mark, Matt, Mercedes, Nicole, Peter, Riccardo, Sheila, Therese and Tom, you are all amazing. We would like to thank the judges – the arbiter of good taste, Patrick Grant, and the inspirational Esme Young for everything they have taught us about what home sewers should aspire to make. A big thank you to our ball of energy of a host, Joe Lycett, who has kept us entertained throughout. For commissioning a sixth series and for all their support, we would like to thank the BBC, particularly David Brindley and Catherine Catton. A final word has to go to the very talented, hardworking team who work behind the scenes on the show. It is their passion and drive that ensures *The Great British Sewing Bee* is the best series it can be... and a nicer bunch of people you could not hope to meet.

ALEXANDRA BRUCE & CAROLINE AKSELSON would like to thank first and foremost Harriet Butt and Emily Lapworth at Quadrille, for making us feel part of a great team, making us feel supported throughout an incredibly tight timeframe and believing in us throughout. Thank you to Sarah Hoggett for being a great copy editor and making our childhood dreams of being authors a legible reality, Hester Llewellyn-Woodward for enthusiastic pattern advice, Jess Chan for her tips on natural dyes, Zuhair at Grade House for taking on our project with a tight deadline, his studio coordinator Christopher who is incredibly speedy at emails, and Harriet Cleary for fabric advice and general life support. Thank you also to the illustrators, Suzie London and Kate Simunek for making our scribbles come to life so beautifully. Thank you to the photographer, Brooke Harwood, the stylist, Charlotte Melling, and the make-up artists, Danni Hooker and Cat Parnell, for bringing the energy and creativity to our vision.

CAROLINE AKSELSON
I would like to thank my family for unfailing support, and my grandparents: my grandmother taught me everything about sewing from the age of five and is the reason I do what I do, and my grandfather was the biggest book lover I have ever known. All my heart to St. Clair and our little baby, who was due at the same time as the book and whose kicks proved the ultimate motivator. And Alexandra, the ultimate other half of my girl boss dreams.

ALEXANDRA BRUCE
I would like to thank my family for always supporting my creative dreams. To my grandmother Olive for inspiring the drive within me to pursue my dreams and for being the ultimate style and feminist icon. To Lee for being a wonderful, loving and caring husband and for ordering take-out most nights! And to Caroline, my best friend and soul sister: I'm so glad we met that day at Wimbledon College of Art or I wouldn't be the woman I am today.

This book is published to accompany the television series entitled *The Great British Sewing Bee*, first broadcast on BBC TWO in 2020.

Executive Producer Sara Ramsden
Series Editor James Hedge
Series Producer Catherine Lewendon
Series Director Justin Lennox-Bradley
Head of Casting Holly Flynn
Producer Jen Greenwood
Sewing Producers Sue Suma, Patrick Thomson
Sewing Assistants Florence Dempster, Fiona Parker, Rachael Maguire and Alice Brown
Production Executive Fin O'Riordan
Production Manager Euan McRae
Director of Legal & Commercial Affairs Rupert Frisby
Publicity Amanda Console and Shelagh Pymm
BBC Commissioning Editor Catherine Catton
BBC Head of Popular Factual & Factual Entertainment
David Brindley

First published in 2020 by Quadrille
an imprint of Hardie Grant Publishing

This US hardback edition published
in 2021 by Quadrille

Quadrille
52–54 Southwark Street
London SE1 1UN
quadrille.com

BBC and the BBC logo are trademarks of the British
Broadcasting Corporation and are used under licence.
BBC logo © BBC 1996
Publishing Director Sarah Lavelle
Commissioning Editor Harriet Butt
Project Editor Sarah Hoggett
Art Director & Designer Emily Lapworth
Photographers Brooke Harwood and Charlotte Medlicott
Stylists Charlotte Melling and Charlie Phillips
Hair & Make-up Cat Parnell and Danni Hooker
Models Anu Elegbede, Chelsea Covington, Jess Rose
Lambregts, Lee Rans, Luke Edmeade, Maia Tassalini,
Suzannah Agrippa, Tatiana Heiss, Wendy
Illustrators Kate Simunek and Suzie London
Pattern Grading Grade House
Makers Deborah Wilkins, Lisa Obuchowska,
Madeleine Jenkins, Susan Young, Twan Lentjes
Testers Amy Scarr, Cat Regalia, Chantelle Collett-Ellis,
Charlotte Powell, Emily Tan, Jenny Joan, Jenny Lingham
Doe, Louise King, Marie Lawlor, Melissa Forrest,
Sarah Boddey, Tyla Thackwray
Alterations Adriane Gaché
Head of Production Stephen Lang
Production Controller Katie Jarvis

British Library Cataloguing-in-Publication Data
A catalogue record for this book is available from
the British Library.

ISBN 978 1 78713 674 8

Printed in China

If you have any comments or queries regarding the
instructions in this book, please contact us at
enquiries@quadrille.co.uk.